Reflections of South African university leaders

1981 to 2014

Published in 2016 by African Minds
4 Eccleston Place, Somerset West, 7130, Cape Town, South Africa
info@africanminds.org.za
www.africanminds.org.za

and

Council on Higher Education (South Africa)
1 Quintin Brand Street, Persequor Technopark, 0020
Tel: +27 12 349 3840
research@che.ac.za
www.che.ac.za

Cite as: Council on Higher Education (2016) *Reflections of South African university
leaders, 1981 to 2014* (African Minds & Council on Higher Education: Cape Town)

ISBN: 978-1-928331-09-4
eBook edition: 978-1-928331-10-0
ePub edition: 978-1-928331-11-7

Copies of this book are available for free download at:
www.africanminds.org.za
www.che.ac.za

ORDERS:
African Minds
Email: info@africanminds.org.za
Or the Council on Higher Education
Email: research@che.ac.za

To order printed books from outside Africa, please contact:
African Books Collective
PO Box 721, Oxford OX1 9EN, UK
Email: orders@africanbookscollective.com

contents

abbreviations and acronyms

AACSB	Association to Advance Collegiate Schools of Business
AARP	Alternative Admissions Research Project
ADP	Academic Development Programme
AMBA	Association of MBAs
ANC	African National Congress
APF	Academic Planning Framework
ASP	Academic Support Programme
ASSAf	Academy of Science of South Africa
ATN	Australian Technology Network
BEE	black economic empowerment
CALICO	Cape Library Consortium
CEO	chief executive officer
CHE	Council on Higher Education
CHEC	Cape Higher Education Consortium
CHED	Centre for Higher Education Development
CPUT	Cape Peninsula University of Technology
CSIR	Council for Scientific and Industrial Research
CUES	Committee on Undergraduate Education in Science
CV	curriculum vitae
DG	director-general
DHET	Department of Higher Education and Training
DUT	Durban University of Technology
DVC	deputy vice-chancellor
EQUIS	European Quality Insurance System
Exco	Executive Committee
FET	further education and training
FRD	Foundation for Research Development
FTE	full-time equivalent

HDI	historically disadvantaged institution
HEQC	Higher Education Quality Committee
HESA	Higher Education South Africa (now Universities South Africa)
HIV/Aids	human immunodeficiency virus/acquired immune deficiency syndrome
HR	human resources
HSRC	Human Sciences Research Council
HWI	historically white institution
ICT	information and communications technology
IIDMM	Institute of Infectious Disease and Molecular Medicine (now the IDM)
IT	information technology
ITV	Independent Television
JET	Joint Education Trust (now JET Education Services)
MEDUNSA	Medical University of South Africa
MIT	Massachusetts Institute of Technology
MK	Umkhonto we Sizwe
MOOCs	Massive Open Online Courses
MP	member of parliament
MRC	Medical Research Council
NACI	National Advisory Council on Innovation
NCHE	National Commission on Higher Education
NDP	National Development Plan
NGO	non-governmental organisation
NMMU	Nelson Mandela Metropolitan University
NQF	National Qualifications Framework
NRF	National Research Foundation
NSFAS	National Student Financial Aid Scheme
NUSAS	National Union of South African Students
PASMA	Pan Africanist Students' Movement of Azania
PE	Port Elizabeth
Pentech	Peninsula Technikon
PET	Port Elizabeth Technikon
PPE	Philosophy, Politics and Economics
PQM	Programme and Qualifications Mix
RSSAf	Royal Society of South Africa
SAAWEK	Suid-Afrikaanse Akademie vir Wetenskap en Kuns
SABC	South African Broadcasting Corporation
SALDRU	Southern Africa Labour and Development Research Unit
SANLAM	Suid-Afrikaanse Nasionale Lewens-Assuransie Maatskappy
SAPSE	South African Post-Secondary Education
SAQA	South African Qualifications Authority

SASCO	South African Students' Congress
SAUVCA	South African Universities Vice-Chancellors' Association
SEASA	Science and Engineering Academy of South Africa
SET	science, engineering and technology
SETA	Sector Education and Training Authority
SGB	standards-generating body
SHAWCO	Students' Health and Welfare Centres Organisation
SLE	senior lecturer equivalent
SRC	Students' Representative Council
STIAS	Stellenbosch Institute for Advanced Study
SU	Stellenbosch University
TB	tuberculosis
TELP	Tertiary Education Linkages Project
TENET	Tertiary Education and Research Network of South Africa
UCT	University of Cape Town
UDUSA	Union of Democratic University Staff Associations
UDW	University of Durban-Westville
UFH	University of Fort Hare
UK	United Kingdom
UNESCO	United Nations Educational, Scientific and Cultural Organization
UNIBO	University of Bophuthatswana
UNISA	University of South Africa
UNITRA	University of Transkei
UNIVEN	University of Venda
UNIZUL	University of Zululand
UPE	University of Port Elizabeth
USA	United States of America
UTF	University Transformation Forum
UWC	University of the Western Cape
VC	vice-chancellor
VCP	vice-chancellor and principal
VRG	Vice-Rectors' Group
WEXDEV	Women Executives Development
Wits	University of the Witwatersrand
WSU	Walter Sisulu University

foreword

Nasima Badsha

Much has been written about the ever-growing demands on university leadership worldwide in the face of increasingly complex changes and challenges from within the academy and beyond. However, as we are reminded by Johan Muller in the Introduction to this book, "there are particular features of time and place that also throw up unique problems". It is precisely 'time and place' that make this set of reflections by university leaders quite remarkable and distinguish it from the many biographies to be found in the literature on higher education leadership. I have had the privilege of working alongside most of these individuals in a range of different capacities, as colleagues in various policy processes in the 1990s and later during my tenure as Deputy Director-General for Higher Education in the former Department of Education from 1997 to 2006.

In the main, this collection spans two decades, the 1990s and 2000s, of unprecedented levels of change in South African higher education. Leaders in universities, as well as those responsible for higher education policy in the government and associated statutory bodies, had no neat script to work off, nor 'manuals' or prescripts of 'good' leadership or practice. Instead, there was palpable excitement about collectively imagining and nurturing a new post-apartheid higher education system, which would contribute to the social and economic development needs of the country and the deepening of democracy, and which would also be globally relevant.

The establishment of the National Commission on Higher Education (NCHE) in 1994 marked the beginning of a period of intense engagement and consultation around the principles and policy frameworks which should shape the new system that was to be carved from a fractured set of individual institutions with disparate histories, capacities, traditions, aims and values. The 1997 *White Paper: A Programme for the Transformation of Higher Education*, and the subsequent Higher Education Act, charted the far-reaching and unprecedented change agenda.

A simple listing of the main changes that were introduced will serve as a reminder of the scope, scale and complexity of the system changes: new management information, funding, planning, governance (institutional and system-wide, including the establishment of the Council on Higher Education [CHE]), quality assurance and reporting systems were introduced. The pressures to deliver on an expanded, more equitable and more responsive higher education system also meant that changes could not be introduced incrementally or in a phased manner. Alongside the changes to the regulatory framework came large-scale institutional restructuring through mergers and incorporations in a bid to fashion a higher education landscape that would (arguably) shed its apartheid legacy and be more responsive to meeting the high-level human resource development needs of the country and assist in the strengthening of scholarship, research and innovation capacity.

It was indeed a tall order, and the extent to which this particular phase in the transformation of higher education succeeded in meeting its stated goals remains a subject of intense contestation. However, it was a key part of the wider context within which higher education leaders were required to operate.

Vice-chancellors (VCs) could no longer confine themselves to looking after the interests of their own institutions but had to juggle these interests (and those of the academy more broadly) with national policy imperatives and the growing expectations of citizens. The individual and collective leadership of university VCs is no doubt central to building strong and sustainable institutions which are part of a robust national system.

There are all too many examples of the consequences of weak leadership, including the number of universities that, at any time, are under administration or in deep and often seemingly perpetual crisis. There are unfortunately many casualties in the recent history of higher education leadership – VCs and other senior executives who, for a myriad of reasons (including some that cannot be directly ascribed to any personal shortcomings of the individuals concerned but could be attributed to various other pressures), were unable to meet the heavy demands of the office.

As we have also seen more recently, the stresses and strains of leadership take their toll on individuals in different ways. A poignant reminder of this is the experience of the late Professor Russel Botman who was the first black VC appointed to head Stellenbosch University in December 2006. He died of a heart attack on 28 June 2014, halfway through his second term in office. By all accounts, the late Professor Russel Botman was a highly regarded, astute and visionary leader of integrity, who, like many of his peers, had to forge an institutional change agenda while navigating the multiple demands and aspirations of different stakeholders. Aspects of his transformation agenda were, however, less than well received in some influential quarters of the University and it is common knowledge that he had been under considerable pressure in the period prior to his untimely death.

It would clearly be naïve to imagine that there is a single view on what transformation means for South African higher education and how it should be measured. In the first two decades of democracy much of the focus was on broadening and diversifying student access. There is much reason to celebrate significant achievements in this area, although much is yet to be achieved, especially in relation to improving quality, student success rates and better pipelines into postgraduate study and research. Less progress has also been made with regard to the renewal of the professoriate, and the representation of black people and women in the senior echelons of the academy remains alarmingly low. These issues remain high on the national agenda.

In the coming years, the higher education leadership in the country will also no doubt be seized with the issues and challenges that are of concern to university leaders worldwide – internationalisation, open-learning technology, marketisation, global rankings and the pressure to deliver more with shrinking resources – to name but a few. Alongside this, they too will confront challenges defined by 'time and place'. As we have been reminded by the recent rise of social movements on a number of campuses, universities in South Africa remain contested spaces. There is renewed debate about what it means to be a university in Africa and how this should shape institutional culture(s), curriculum and scholarship more broadly, and about how universities and students should be funded. This is part of the complex terrain within which university executives are expected to lead and manage. As is evident from many of the journeys recalled in this book, the ride is likely to be bumpy, but not without its rewards.

I highly recommend this collection of reflections from men and women who have had the privilege of shaping their universities in defining moments of history. Their stories are testaments to their resilience.

July 2015

introduction

Johan Muller

The inspiration for this collection arose in late 2013 in the Council on Higher Education's (CHE) Monitoring and Evaluation Directorate, the Directorate responsible for conducting research on the higher education landscape and monitoring the state of the sector over time. The Directorate noted that conditions besetting universities had grown increasingly complex, both globally and, more especially, locally, and the question arose as to how this had altered the challenges to university leadership over the period, say, between the new political dispensation ushered in in 1994 and the second decade of the new millennium. More particularly, how had leaders with a proven track record of visionary and strong leadership during this period faced these challenges? How did they see the main changes that needed dealing with? What challenges did these changes pose and how were they successfully overcome? What did they think, looking back, were the main constituents of successful leadership and management? What wisdom could be distilled for posterity?

The Directorate decided to invite a range of vice-chancellors (VCs) and senior academic leaders who had completed their terms of office to contribute to a project that set out to gather such reflections and compile them into a publication. The publication was intended to serve not only as a resource for present and future leaders, but also to stand as a personal record of a turbulent and eventful landscape successfully negotiated. The format for the reflection could take one of two forms: it could either be a concise, self-drafted reflection, or it could take the form of a recorded interview with Denyse Webbstock and Neo Lekgotla *laga* Ramoupi. These interviews were later transcribed by Ramoupi and the collection as a whole was edited by Johan Muller and Ramoupi.

While a number of individuals were approached, many were not able to participate for a range of personal reasons. Of those who participated, four undertook to write a reflection for the publication and four consented to an interview. With the exception of Professor Saunders, whose incumbency covered the 1980s and five years of the 1990s, this collection represents leaders whose reflections largely cover the 1990s (Professors Gevers, Gourley, Figaji and Brink)[1] and 2000s (Professors Brink, Stumpf, Nongxa, Tanga, and, briefly, Gevers and Figaji). This gives a spread of leadership experience which includes experience in institutions in the Eastern Cape, Western Cape, Gauteng and KwaZulu-Natal, as well as reflections from two VCs who had also accumulated significant international experience, namely Professors Gourley and Brink. The publication covers different university types and orientations, from research-intensive institutions to comprehensives, and from universities of technology to merged institutions. At least three of the accounts touch on mergers, sometimes in passing, sometimes at length (Professors Figaji, Stumpf and Tanga).

It would, undoubtedly, have been preferable to be able to reflect more of a race and gender balance, but, as the extended reflection on gender issues in Professor Tanga's chapter shows, with few exceptions, women have only recently begun to participate at senior levels of university leadership in the country. The same is true with respect to race. This signifies not only lost opportunities but probably loss of efficiency too, if recent research on the 'diversity dividend' has application to higher education.[2] It would also have been preferable to have had more of a geographical spread of experiences, but availability and inclination proved the determining factors in the final selection. There is no sense, then, in which this publication is representative, or indeed had intentions of being fully representative. Nevertheless, as the reader will no doubt see, the spread of experiences raises many intriguing points for comparison.

There are myriad sound decisions to be made daily to keep the complex organisation of a university operating smoothly at the best of times, let alone in turbulent times. The reflections see Professor Nongxa worrying about finances, Brink about quality, Gevers about the curriculum and Figaji about academic values, to take random examples. All of these issues are perennial issues for universities, but

---

1   The collection is ordered chronologically, based on the date when the incumbent took up the post under discussion.
2   See, for example: Joffe, H. (2015) 'Women at JCE make the case for diversity dividend' in *Business Day*, 11 March.

all of them are affected by changes in the political and policy environment. Academic values are put under strain when universities are expected to be run like businesses, or when universities are expected to greatly expand in size. Demand for increased access to higher education, a major imperative in the post-transition period, is an underlying motif of many of the new pressures these leaders faced. Before the transition, the imperative to extend access was principally political and ethical, as Professor Saunders' chapter reflects; after transition, it also becomes an issue of quality (Brink), and dealing with increasing diversity (Figaji and Tanga), a theme threading through many of the chapters.

Together with the perennial issues of university leadership and management, and the ways in which these become more complex and multipronged as the political and policy environment grows more complex, there are the particular features of time and place that also throw up unique problems. There is no single right way of dealing with these, and different styles of approach are noticeable. Some approach the task strategically and map out a set of priorities and action plans; others conceive of levels of engagement; yet others approach the immediate tasks more intuitively, trusting to integrity to see them through. On display here are versions of the scholar–leader, the visionary leader, the leader from the business sector, the strategic planner, and many others in various combinations. Sometimes these styles are explicit; more often they are implicit.

The value of an efficient administrative base is mentioned by some, not by others. For some it is an asset that had to be hard-won; others scarcely mention it, perhaps because it has long been in place. In this way the different legacies of the institutions also speak through these accounts.

One virtue of these reflections is that they show leadership to be an essentially situated expertise. The stories they relate are fascinating and revealing not because they lay bare an essential leadership exoskeleton of skills necessary for success in all times and in all places, although there are clear general lessons to be drawn here. They are valuable rather for what they tell us about the times, the institution, the leadership characteristics of the ex-incumbents, about their special passions and their foibles. This is to say, these accounts, in all their richness, show leadership to be an open-hearted human calling, fatefully situated in a determinate history, in an actual institution, amongst all-too-human colleagues. These reflections reveal what leadership is when it lives and breathes, which is far removed from leadership conceived as a bloodless generic skill set, distilled into ten bullet points or offered as a magic wand. That it is also intensely moral comes through with force and clarity. These leaders all did their level best by their moral lights and precepts, which is the point where the reflections largely converge. The necessity for unwavering honesty and integrity comes through time and again.

Another virtue of these reflections is the immediacy of the voice, certainly in the interviews, but also at times in the essays penned for publication. The interviews are necessarily in the first person, often also the present tense. Even when the ex-incumbent does reminisce in the past tense, the editors were struck by how, in the midst of the recollection, engagement in this or that issue is triggered anew, and the speech, sometimes even the prose, slipped into the present tense, as if the reminiscence had drawn them back into the thick of things. At these moments, the reader becomes aware how intimately these events, sometimes recalled decades afterwards, are living issues for these protagonists. For some, preserving distance is important, but others re-enter the debate and argue the case anew. In editing these voices, the editors have inevitably smoothed out some of the more idiosyncratic features, but have endeavoured in all cases to preserve the unique timbre of each individual voice.

When reading these reflections and recollections, it pays to bear in mind that these are the reflections of people who are in the first instance leaders, not dispassionate scholars of higher education. Some of them are that too, as the chapters will reveal, and readers will discern in places the mediated analytical voice of academic leadership. Being a leader, however, does not require being able to reflect upon one's role in an academic mode. Leaders are by definition women and men of action, people who have to make decisions rapidly, seize the moment, and make things happen. When asked a general question, as they were in the interviews for example, they were apt to respond in terms of a specific event or incident, which they expect the reader to grasp as standing for a class of incidents. These reflections may thus seem at first like biographical musings, but it is between the lines that other meanings also lie.

There are some who may be inclined to disparage the biographical mode as 'mere musing' – personal memories fondly recollected. The reader of these reflections may well come to a different conclusion. Hindsight may be selective, but that is its strength. What hindsight selects from a vast store of experiences can be instructive – which events and issues to single out for special mention or attention. These re-'views' are also necessarily 'one-sided', expressing the result of the encounter between a general problem refracted through the history of a particular institution and its particular participants on the one hand, and the point of decision reached by someone approaching the problem from their own unique cultural and academic careers on the other hand. In this way, these reflections refract the interplay between general challenges to, and characteristics of, leadership, and the personal decision arrived at with its determinate consequences. All these consequences taken together constitute a definable legacy, and it is this legacy, spoken as it were from the inside, that these reflections display and that contribute to the legacy of each of their institutions.

Not all the stories here deal with success, and from these too there are lessons to be drawn. There are missteps, though not too many, as one would expect. More striking, though, is that the accounts will confidently advance views that are different from the views taken, explicitly or implicitly, by their peers. This should not occasion a loss of confidence. These views only fully make sense when considered in the context of a coherent style of leadership, each of which can be successful under the right circumstances. Which is not to say that anything goes. Rather, it underscores the fact that successful leaders all have a coherent style, which becomes more than the sum of its parts, and it is these styles that are on display in these gripping and instructive accounts.

Each chapter opens with a brief biography. The idea was that each should reflect the academic origins and destinations of the ex-incumbents, but the participants had their own ideas about how they wanted to present themselves. Some of them prefer the brief, pithy and impersonal entry; others wish the reader to have some insight into where they came from, what formed their ideas, and to see the past that shaped the particular trajectory of this university leader. We respected these choices. What can be seen, however, is that most of these ex-incumbents, having risen to public prominence and responsibility in the university, have remained in public life in one way or the other, and continue to make significant contributions to their academic or professional peers, or to the public at large. This is validation, were it needed, that each of these people has made, and continues to make, a contribution beyond normal expectation.

Most reflections touch on the coalface of leadership, which is the face-to-face interactional dimension: dealing with staff, with students, with council chairs. What comes through clearly is the importance of what are sometimes called 'people skills'. In these accounts this is not simply presented as a human relations aptitude, for a number of reasons, first of which is the special nature of universities and their occupants. More than one points out the special challenge of managing the talented people that are academics, and their inbuilt distaste for bureaucracy, and their reluctance to be managed or told what to do. The message here is consistently one of needing to be completely open with academics, the importance of maintaining the distinction between 'collegial' and 'executive' management (avoiding 'managerialism'), and the critical importance of winning and holding their trust.

Holding the trust of students is also critical as these accounts show. It is noteworthy how positively disposed these ex-VCs are to students, still today, bearing in mind that they frequently had to deal with student protests and challenges to their authority. Managing positive relations with their councils and their council chairs also seems to be key, and happy is the VC who has cordial and productive relations with the chair of council. Above all, the successful leader must, at times, 'take the heat', not pass the buck, and represent the authority of the institution fully.

Many other themes criss-cross these accounts: the importance, but difficulty, of changing 'mindsets'; and learning to resist pressure from outside in the running of the institution, to mention two. There are also special events that challenge some institutions, not others; the most momentous in these accounts probably being how to steer a course through a merger successfully. This is only to scratch the surface of this rich collection.

Doctors Webbstock and Ramoupi had worked out a list of topics that they wished the participants to cover. However, it was soon clear that there were certain topics that appealed to the participants more than others and it is in the reflections on these topics that the richness of these accounts lies. We trust that you will find much food for fruitful reflection in these accounts, singly and taken together. We invite you to contact us with any reflections you may care to share.

chapter 1

The challenges of politics and collegial relations

Stuart Saunders

Professor Stuart John Saunders was the seventh Vice-Chancellor (VC) of the University of Cape Town (UCT), from January 1981 to August 1996, serving a period of 15 years.

He was born in Cape Town on 28 August 1931. After graduating from UCT with an MBChB with honours in 1953, he undertook postgraduate research at the Royal Postgraduate Medical School at Hammersmith in London and at Harvard University. He received the degree of Doctor of Medicine in 1965 from UCT. He began his administrative career as UCT's Head of the Department of Medicine (1971–1980) and was co-founder of the University's Liver Clinic and Liver Research Unit, a field in which he wrote over 200 articles and co-authored a study that has become a classical reference work.

His 15 years as VC included some of the darkest days of apartheid and the dramatic changes which brought it to an end. There were states of emergency; severe erosions of academic freedom, freedom of association and freedom of speech; and direct attacks by government on the University. Saunders also served in the National Working Group established by the South African Minister of Education to look at the restructuring of higher education in 2001; served on the Council on Higher Education (CHE) from 2002 to 2010; and was the Deputy Chairperson of the CHE from 2008 to 2010.

Saunders is credited with putting an end to the racially segregated training of medical registrars and for admitting students of all races to UCT's residences; for initiating fundraising among South African universities so as to ensure their academic freedom; and with meaningful service to science and to the nation.

This chapter is based on an interview conducted by Denyse Webbstock and Neo Lekgotla laga Ramoupi on 9 May 2014 in Cape Town.

Academic leadership in higher education institutions has become increasingly challenging in rapidly changing global realities and is all the more complex in South Africa. South African academic institutions have been privileged to have had many visionary and strong leaders in the period of transition from apartheid and in the first two decades of democracy. Such leaders were faced with enhancing the quality of the higher education system and with pursuing the goals of equity and redress, while at the same time managing institutions that were themselves undergoing structural and other far-reaching changes. Many of these leaders are now retired, or are busy with different activities. Hindsight is instructive. Distance allows deep and wise reflection on the lessons learnt and on the nature of academic leadership and the way in which leadership is affected by different contexts, and provides an opportunity to consider what was achieved and what might have been.

Stuart Saunders' academic background is in medicine. He is a physician by training and was a professor of medicine at the Medical School of the University of Cape Town (UCT) from 1971 to 1980. His term of office as Vice-Chancellor (VC) of UCT started on 5 January 1981 after acting as assistant Principal (Deputy Vice-Chancellor) on a part-time basis from April 1977. At the time, Richard Luyt was the VC of the University.

Saunders enjoyed his interaction with the students as a professor, which begs the question as to why he left teaching and entered into leadership and administration. He explains how he allowed his name to go forward as a candidate for the vice-chancellorship because he could see the threats that the University faced from the Nationalist government, and he did not have the confidence that the other candidates, whom he knew, would have defended the University in the way in which he thought it ought to be defended. Therefore, he left medicine, reluctantly, but he did so without regrets. He remained in touch with the profession and he has worked as a physician until quite recently.

Saunders cites two experiences that profoundly moulded his preparation to occupy the office of the Vice-Chancellor. One was the Leo Marquard papers:

> After I had been appointed, but before I had taken up the position,
> I was preparing my inaugural address, and I read the Leo Marquard
> papers. He was the founder of the National Union of South African
> Students (NUSAS) and of the Liberal Party. He was a patient of mine;
> I knew him well. Marquard was a member of the UCT Council, and
> I greatly admired him. I read the correspondence between him and

Monica Wilson, Professor of Social Anthropology at UCT. Monica described to Marquard when Richard Luyt became the VC of UCT and chaired the Senate, how his qualities of leadership transformed the Senate and gave it direction and purpose. That focused my mind on how important leadership was for a VC in a university. Of course, it is important for anyone in the comparable position, but that underlined it for me.

The second experience was a conversation he had had with the Dean of the Medical School of the Ben-Gurion University who had visited Cape Town, and who had come to see him when Saunders was still a professor of medicine at UCT:

> When you become a head of a department of medicine, you have to put aside your personal research ambitions, not completely, but you have to downscale them; and you have to put the department first and members of the department, students and postgraduate students first. That was your job. And it is the same when you become a VC, you have to put the university first, and the staff and students first, not your ambitions and the promotion of yourself.

The position of VC, he told us, was not one that a person should occupy for a short period of time only:

> I think a VC has to have five years at least. Those who come and leave quickly damage the university and undermine any legacy they might have had. Ideally, the person who wants to be a VC should have an academic background, but it does not always have to be the case. Richard Luyt did not come from academia, and he provided very good academic leadership, so it is not essential.[1] Luyt recognised his shortcomings in the academic area. It is best if somebody has been a head of department, dean or deputy VC, or has been active in research, because then they are more likely to enjoy the respect of the academic staff and the students.
> One thing that is crucial is consistency. If one says one is going to do something, do it. Never make a promise which one cannot keep. Always keep your word; without that, it is difficult to provide good leadership. I will also say one should not spend the university's money on yourself. One must avoid the Nkandla syndrome! The dignity of the post does mean it is appropriate to do some things. One must avoid expensive

---

1   Richard Luyt was Saunders' predecessor as UCT Vice-Chancellor.

cars, frequent overseas visits, travelling first class. Those kinds of events undermine one's leadership. I think one has to know the staff well, and I think to give good leadership one has to visit all departments regularly, listen to what they have to say, and know what is happening on the campus. That allows one to give leadership, and act.

Managerialism in universities

There are different styles of leadership, said Saunders. He preferred collegial relations in the University rather than a managerial style. He explains:

Margaret Thatcher introduced the form of managerialism that is to be found in universities throughout the world, throughout South Africa. South Africans are, by and large, not in favour of it. I think it is much better to have deans who are elected by faculties, and are responsible to faculties, rather than executive deans appointed by councils. To give proper leadership one must be on top of the finances of the university, and play an important role in their allocations. One must be prepared to fundraise because without that the university will have a great deal of difficulty in managing finances. One must defend the independence of the university; the academic freedom of staff and students [is] absolutely crucial. One has to be able to take the heat in the kitchen. I know of some VCs in other universities who could not take the heat in the kitchen, and that is a disaster. One has to have the right instincts – that is crucial in a crisis. If there is an unwarranted attack on the university, one must act with vigour; don't duck for cover. One can tell how good a VC is by how they respond to a crisis. One must not seek the limelight, and one must not pontificate on things one knows little about. A leader must have vision, must anticipate change. Barack Obama has shown that; one cannot doubt his great leadership. Of course he's had great political difficulties, but one cannot doubt his leadership. One cannot be a leader if one just sits behind one's desk. One of the problems I think we have is that people who are appointed, not only at universities but also in government positions and in other places, think that is it. They think they have to sit behind the desk and other people will do the work. One has to work hard; one cannot be a good leader if one doesn't work very hard, and one must be completely involved in and informed about every aspect of the institution. Len Abrahamse, who was the Chairman of the UCT Council for a large part of the time when I was VC, had an expression which I think comes from Shakespeare, because he was a Shakespeare scholar, though I have not been able to find it.

He used to say, 'As is the King, so are the people', which is wise.[2] That is what Monica Wilson was referring to about Leo Marquard.

Saunders was clear about the right way to manage and relate to staff:

> A good leader in the university does not deal with staff as though they were petty criminals. Someone does something wrong, one has to deal with it, but one should also respect what they say. One may disagree with them profoundly, but one must show respect and respect their right to say it. I have been appalled by the uncollegial, non-disciplinary way that some people have been treated on occasion in universities.

Saunders believes that, with the advent of the Internet and globalisation, and with everything being so connected as a consequence, it would not have been possible to escape managerialism. When he left UCT in the late 1990s, the institution still had collegial relations, but it was clear to him, even then, that the University was moving towards managerialism, almost inevitably. He remembers that there were meetings about it. The deans thought that it would be much better for them, but he objected to it, for the following reasons:

> The relationship between deans and the academic staff was not a collegial one because the deans had to instruct their academic staff. One of the problems was that each faculty received its budget, and they were responsible for staffing, amongst other recurrent costs. Unless the university reserved some money in a central pool, it was very difficult to initiate cooperative enterprises between faculties. One had to be able to do new things that cut across faculties. It did happen, but it was limited by silos of money in faculties.

It is a fact that, when a university becomes more like a business, the relationships change. Sometime in the future the pendulum will swing back in a lot of institutions. Saunders believes that the only institutions that will endure are the Church and the universities, although he knew a lot of people would disagree with him on this point. He always maintained that apartheid would go one day, but two things would remain: the Cathedral and UCT.

---

2   The basic sentiment is found in the sayings of many cultures. The oldest is perhaps the Sanskrit 'Yatha Raja, Tatha Praja' (As the King, so the people), but it is also found in Latin sayings and in the Bible, *Isaiah* 24:2.

In the 1980s, the universities received financial threats from the Nationalist government. This was the only threat they experienced as far as the main business of the university was concerned. This came as a consequence of universities protesting against the state of emergency, apartheid and racism. The Nationalists had said that, if the universities did not stop their protests, they would cut their subsidies. UCT, in particular, took the state to the Supreme Court and won the case. During that time Saunders remembers being told by a VC of another English-speaking university that he was mad to take the state to court. This VC said his university council had said that the VC of UCT was acting irresponsibly. Saunders recalled that this took place in about 1989 or 1990, not long before the release of Nelson Mandela.

In retrospect, Saunders thought it was surprising that the Nationalist government did not interfere more often with the core business of the universities. The ruling party did indeed interfere when they stopped the UCT Council from appointing Archie Mafeje to the position of senior lecturer in the Department of Social Anthropology. The government said that, if the University appointed him, a black academic, they would be forced to pass a law to the effect that the government would vet every appointment in every university in South Africa. Saunders recounted that the Council succumbed to government pressure, and did not appoint Mafeje.

> UCT got a lot of criticism for that decision. I understand that view. I was not involved with the Mafeje affair at all, as I was a professor of medicine at the time, but it was not an easy decision for the Council. They did not want the government to approve every appointment in the university. That was direct interference. Of course, the establishment of apartheid in higher education was direct interference. But apart from those very fundamental things, on day-to-day things, they interfered very little. Universities in South Africa had more independence than many universities elsewhere. I think that tradition has continued, though I am not close enough to be certain, since I left in 1996. I only had two years of Mandela's government. We had excellent relations with Mandela. I saw some of government from the inside when I sat on the National Working Group, and at that time I did not see any tendency to interfere inappropriately in universities. I am not quite as confident now, but I don't have any hard facts to back that up. The VCs of this country have to be alert to protect their institutions against any tendencies to interfere inappropriately in them.

The 'excellent relations with Mandela' that Saunders alluded to are traceable back to the end of 1989. UCT had decided, while Mandela was still in prison at Victor Verster in Paarl, that it would honour him with an honorary doctorate in law. Saunders wrote Mandela a letter on 8 December 1989 informing him of UCT's intention to confer this degree upon him. Mandela replied to say that he would be honoured to receive an honorary degree from the UCT. Saunders had chaired a committee at UCT that consisted of representatives from all segments of the University, including the students and the trade union, and the African National Congress (ANC), to plan the ceremony at which the honorary degree would be conferred. Saunders remembered that Mandela received the honorary degree at a specially arranged ceremony on UCT's main rugby field in front of the oldest buildings of the University, at 4:30pm on Friday, 30 November 1990, making UCT one of the very first universities to honour Nelson Mandela, even before he became the President of both the ANC and South Africa.

Saunders related an example of the kind of outside pressure a head of department, or even a VC of a university, can experience from the public. During his vice-chancellorship people who wanted their child to get into the medical school would contact him, and he said he had a standard answer for them: "My own son could not get into medical school, and I did nothing about it"; that silenced them.[3] The rationale for this refusal, Saunders felt, underlined the fact that UCT's admission procedures were fair and it turned out to be a trump card down the years for the deans of medicine and for Saunders when dealing with irate parents whose children had failed to gain admission.

Academic leadership

We asked Saunders to reflect on his experiences of academic leadership:

> I have reflected on the academic leadership that I have seen in other institutions; it is very hard to reflect on oneself. Let me give you an occurrence that comes to mind. In the National Working Group we had detailed financial analyses of all the universities in the country.

---

3   Saunders, S. (2000) *Vice-Chancellor on a Tightrope: A Personal Account of Climactic Years in South Africa* (David Philip: Cape Town), p.96; At the time, his son, John, was at Abbots College, and did not qualify for entry into the medical school at UCT. He decided to repeat his matric to improve his school-leaving marks so that he could qualify for medical school, but, in the end, decided he no longer wanted to go to medical school: "Some have expressed surprise that my son could not get into our medical school, but I have never believed that one should 'pull strings' for one's children."

We could see that the University of the Western Cape (UWC) under its then-VC was heading for insolvency. We were told that if the winds were favourable at UWC, we might just survive, but if the winds were in the slightest bit adverse, the University would go bankrupt. We recommended that UWC merge with Cape Technikon. In the event, I think because of political pressure, they did not merge. Cape Tech went on to merge with Peninsula Tech to form the Cape Peninsula University of Technology (CPUT), and a new VC was appointed to head UWC. He gave superb leadership and turned the University around. By the 2000s, it was financially secure. It is now a very good university. That was the result of the VC's leadership. He was clear in his aims that the UWC would survive; he was confident, he gave confidence to his staff, he paid attention to the students and their needs, and he fundraised very successfully to add to the finances. One can see their new Science Building. That is one of the tangible fruits of the academic leadership of the VC; he actually saved the university. If they had appointed someone who was not a good leader, who didn't have a clear idea of where he or she was going, did not know what he or she was doing, they would have gone down the tubes. That is the best academic reflection I can give you.

Having achieved that immense success in saving UWC as an institution, it was really regrettable, said Saunders, that the VC's term of office had come to an end rather messily, which is so often the result of institutional governance.[4] This reminded Saunders about the time when he was appointed VC of UCT:

When I was appointed, I was 48 years old and they wanted to appoint me until 65. I refused because I did not think it was healthy for the institution. I mean, I knew of cases in this country where VCs had no compulsory retirement age and they were finding it difficult to get rid of them. So I insisted on a five-year contract that could be renewed. But if at any time I had lost the confidence of the Council and all the students for justifiable reasons, I would resign. Part of my contract said I could go back to the medical school as a full professor of medicine with no administrative duties at the end of my VC contract. That was the deal. I was there for 16 years as a result of that deal. The Chairman of the University Council played a crucial role. He had to give leadership

4   Thamm, M. (2014) 'The life of Brians: What the hell is going on at UWC?' in *Daily Maverick*, 11 June. From http://www.dailymaverick.co.za/article/2014-06-11-the-life-of-brians-what-the-hell-is-going-on-at-uwc/#.VClaFtgcQfg. Accessed 6 August 2015.

to the Council and also had to be supportive of the VC. I was extremely lucky in the person of Len Abrahamse, who had been a Chairman of Shell. He was the person who created Nedbank. He was a remarkable man. There were occasions when I took the decision to do something in conflict with the government that Len was not sure about and he used to say to me, "I hear you. Go ahead." He never said to me, "Don't do that", even though I know at times he had reservations. Judge Diemont was conservative, but he also always supported me. The chairman of council must never try to run the university. We had another chairman subsequently, whose relationship with me was always very good. But if I was away and someone else was in charge, he tried to run the show, and that was a mistake. The chairman of council is important in giving support to the VC, but must not try to do the VC's job. Councils are very important. I think the problem with some current university councils is that sometimes the members don't understand their roles; they don't always understand what the university is all about.

Opening of UCT's residences to black students

In 1997, Saunders was succeeded by Mamphele Ramphele, the first black South African woman to hold the position of Vice-Chancellor at UCT and at a South African academic institution. Writing in the fore-word of her predecessor's memoirs, Ramphele said:

> The Saunders legacy to higher education is not just tied to the dynamic leadership he gave to making the University of Cape Town an innovator in teaching and research over a period of over sixteen years, but to the dogged way in which he pushed the boundaries of an apartheid state to create space for higher education to rise to its responsibilities. The opening of UCT's residences to black students might today look too ordinary to warrant special mention, but taken in the context of the day it was an act of courage. It was not only taking on the State, but also challenging the many ordinary white Capetonians who paid lip-service to non-racialism.[5]

In her own memoirs, Ramphele wrote a chapter on higher education in which she stressed Saunders' exemplary role among the leaders of higher education in the early 1990s:

---

5   Ramphele, M. (2000) 'Foreword' in Saunders, *Vice-Chancellor on a Tightrope*.

[Saunders] took a personal interest in transformation and attended the UTF [University Transformation Forum] workshops. Students respected him because he cared deeply about their welfare and that of the institution. Saunders had been one of the first leaders of higher education to find loopholes in the apartheid legislation to open access to UCT's residence to black students and to raise funds to provide financial support for poor talented students.[6]

The Group Areas Act of 1950 established residential and business areas according to different racial groups, and prevented blacks from encroaching on what apartheid legislation proclaimed as 'white areas'. According to this Act, black students in universities designated for whites were not allowed to live in the residences with their white counterparts. However, when Saunders became the VC in 1981, he felt it was important for UCT to demonstrate non-racialism, which led to the epithet of UCT being a non-racial island in a sea of racism.[7] The University had admitted its first small group of black students in the 1920s, but the number of black students started to increase in the 1980s.[8]

The integration of the residences at UCT, on the whole, started in 1981. The life experiences and cultural values of the black students were usually distinct from those of the white students. The value of formal house dinners and other 'traditions' in residences were questioned and a great deal of discussion and tolerance was needed by all; the senior students, wardens and sub-wardens all played important roles, and, while there were some problems, Saunders felt that none had become major and all had been resolved within the 'house'. It was the conviction of the VC that UCT, and particularly its residences, should be places where students of different backgrounds could live, learn, and play together and that this would be a major contribution to the new South Africa. UCT also began to enrol increasing numbers of black students – from less than 10 per cent in the 1970s, black student enrolments grew to over a third of the University's student body by 1993.[9]

6   Ramphele, M. (2008) *Laying the Ghosts to Rest: Dilemmas of Transformation in South Africa* (Tafelberg: Cape Town), p.214.
7   Saunders, *Vice-Chancellor on a Tightrope*, p.226.
8   'Our history'. From https://www.uct.ac.za/about/intro/history/. Accessed 6 August 2015.
9   Luescher, T.M. (2009) 'Racial desegregation and the institutionalisation of "race" in university governance: The case of the University of Cape Town,' in *Perspectives in Education*, 27(4), December, p.415.

At the same time that UCT's residences were opened to black students, more white students sought accommodation and lived off-campus. Saunders gives a combination of three reasons for their exodus. First, fashions change and, at times, living in private homes close to campus became highly desirable. Secondly, the cost of residential accommodation on campus could be higher in any one year than off-campus housing. Thirdly, some parents of new white students and returning students and the students themselves may have been unenthusiastic about UCT's policy of integrating the residences.[10]

According to the VC, the third reason was the least important, because no parent or student expressed that view to him. However, silence on the matter does not mean the issue does not exist, and he thought that they would not express such a blatantly racial matter because that would have made them racists publicly. The main complaint the white students and their parents brought to the VC was that the black students were getting preference with regard to accommodation. Saunders explained that, to some degree, that was true, because the black students' need was much greater – the University could persuade few householders in surrounding suburbs to give them lodgings, while white students were easily accepted simply because of their race. The University was criticised for this by some out-of-town white parents who refused to allow their children to come to UCT because the institution would not accommodate them on campus; and they were critical of UCT's residence-admission policy.[11]

Black students were not the only group affected by the Group Areas Act. Black staff also experienced problems with housing. As a result of this Act, the University held title to houses in 'white areas' that had been 'bought' by black staff members in the late 1980s. There was a binding agreement that, if that staff member wished to sell the house, all the proceeds reverted to him or her in exactly the same way as if they had held title. Fortunately, complaints from white neighbours were sent to the Attorney-General for action and not dealt with directly by the police, as had been the case in the past. There were a number of such complaints. Each time, Saunders said he phoned Mr Rossouw, the Attorney-General, and each time he said the file would fall off his table and that no action would be taken! In terms of the Group Areas Act, each 'population' group or 'race' had to live in its 'own' area. Saunders recounted the tale of one of UCT's black members of staff who lived on

---

10 Saunders, *Vice-Chancellor on a Tightrope*, p.226.
11 Ibid.

a road which formed the boundary between the coloured and white areas in Woodstock. His wife was expecting another child and there was an ideal house with additional accommodation for sale on the opposite side of the road, but, because it fell within the white group area, they were not allowed to live there. They could not cross the road! Saunders appealed to the Administrator, Gene Louw, but he would not help.[12]

Community engagement

We asked Saunders to recount his experience with community engagement during his term of office at UCT:

> I always thought the University had to stick to its main business of research and teaching, but also be responsive to the community around it. I thought that the annual Summer School was very important. One of the aims of the School was to reach the working people of the city at all levels, but it was not easy for many of them to get out to the campus during the day. So we had seminars and programmes in the communities; in all the communities around the University. A lot of the research work done at UCT has consequences for the communities around the University. At UCT there is a student organisation called SHAWCO [Students' Health and Welfare Centres Organisation] that is deeply involved in the community with food schemes, educational schemes, social work, old age, rape crisis, and those kinds of things. Through SHAWCO, the University is trying to help children in Langa, Khayalitsha, and Nyanga, whose schools are often not well staffed or [are] short-staffed. All these things I think are important, but a university that spends 80 per cent of its time on those kinds of activities is not a university, even though I think a university has to be involved in those activities.

Tertiary Education Network

Saunders was the founder and first chairman of the Tertiary Education and Research Network of South Africa (TENET). We asked him to tell us how he got involved with it. He explains:

> South Africa's universities' connectivity to the Internet was originally through Rhodes [University], but was taken over by the NRF [National Research Foundation]. It was costing them two million rand a year.

---

12 Ibid., p.227.

They decided that they were going to close it down. That was the one thing. The other thing was that Atlantic Philanthropies and the Mellon Foundation decided to computerise the management of all the libraries of all the universities and research councils in South Africa; and they did that. But in the process, they discovered that the bandwidth was too small and the costs too high. They cornered me in New York and said they wanted me to solve the problem. I told them I didn't know anything about the Internet, except that I used it; in other words, what the average person knew. When I returned I formed a small committee. We met with top management of Telkom, which had a monopoly, and after about three years we got a deal with Telkom that gave universities and research councils a lower price for the service. That worked satisfactorily for some time. We formed TENET and the universities collectively appointed the directors of TENET. I insisted from the start that nobody would be paid, except for the chief executive, the chief financial officer and the staff, who were well paid. I decided I was going to stand down as Chairman. Although we did not have any problems with government, I did not think it was right for the chair to be a white male, so I stood down, and Loyiso Nongxa replaced me.[13] Before that, one of the VCs contacted me to indicate his interest in the chairmanship. When he found out that it was unpaid, he lost interest.

TENET then bought into the undersea cable SEACOM and the universities and research councils got fair service from TENET, which was controlled by the universities. I was taken out to dinner by the Director-General of the Department of Science and Technology who said that the National Research Network had to do for the country what TENET had done for higher education. He wanted us to be part of government. We refused because we knew that would make us disappear. In the end, they formed a structure at the Council for Scientific and Industrial Research [CSIR] that worked together with TENET; but TENET has not disappeared. I know all the jargon, I can talk it, but I don't really know anything about it. The people that I worked with were the experts. They knew everything about information technology.

Constituencies

We asked the VC which he found to be the most challenging constituencies to work with:

---

13 Loyiso Nongxa, later to become the VC of Wits University.

When I was interviewed for my appointment, I was asked by Francis Wilson how I thought I would deal with students.[14] I said, "I have been a warden for a students' residence for 16 years", and I thought I had seen everything that students can do. But I was wrong. I think one of the big challenges of governing universities is to meet the challenges posed by very bright young people who are thinking out of the box; it is very exciting. I really enjoyed the interaction with students. Quite often, somebody comes up to me, we would chat, and they would apologise for what they had done as a student. I am consistent with my answer; I say, "It was your role, don't apologise!" There is one individual who really gave me uphill, who is now a very prominent academic in this country. We met recently and he said to me, "I am sure you don't know who I am"; and I said to him, "I know exactly who you are." He said, "Well I gave you some problems." I said to him, "Don't worry about that – that was your job." I didn't approve of it at the time. But, you know, that is it.

The most interesting challenge is the one presented by the young minds. Students are great!

Conclusion

Finally, we asked Saunders whether, in hindsight, there was something he would have done differently:

> I was involved in protests and marching against the apartheid state and so on. But I think we could have been more effective there, in the political sphere, not the university's sphere. During the state of emergency, I don't think the government would have attacked us. I think they were too frightened to attack us. So there we could have done more. I think we did not do enough in the political sphere to challenge and protest against the government of the day.

At the end of their term, every leader looks back and analyses his or her leadership of the institution. The achievements that Saunders cites as those of which he is most proud at UCT, relate to the uncertainties of the times. The thing that gave him the greatest fulfilment was not to do with academic matters; he said he was very pleased with

---

14 Professor Francis Wilson taught for over 30 years in the School of Economics (UWC), where he founded the Southern Africa Labour and Development Research Unit (SALDRU). https://www.saldru.uct.ac.za/people/honorary-research-associates. Accessed 6 August 2015.

the way UCT had developed. What gave him the greatest satisfaction was the way that the University stood up against the injustices of the apartheid system. In retrospect, that is always how one sees things: "We could have done more."

chapter 2

Helping to lead a university:
A job not what it seems

Wieland Gevers

Professor Wieland Gevers was Deputy Vice-Chancellor (DVC) of the University of Cape Town (UCT) from 1990 to 2002, first in an acting capacity for two years; and then for five years with responsibility for academic affairs. Thereafter, he was Senior DVC for a further period of six years.

He was born in Piet Retief (now eMkhondo) in 1937, and studied medicine at UCT until 1960 (graduating with first-class honours), before moving to Oxford University to obtain a DPhil in Biochemistry in 1966. After a postdoctoral period at Rockefeller University in New York, he returned to South Africa in 1970 as Professor of Medical Biochemistry and Director of a Medical Research Council (MRC) unit at Stellenbosch University. He became a professor, in the same discipline, at UCT in 1978, directing another MRC research unit, before becoming acting DVC.

Wieland Gevers was the prime mover in starting a number of organisations, amongst them the South African Society of Biochemistry and Molecular Biology, the Cape Higher Education Consortium, the Academy of Science of South Africa, and the UCT Institute for Infectious Disease and Molecular Medicine. Among the numerous awards he has received are those from: the South African Society for Biochemistry and Molecular Biology; the South African MRC; the Southern African Association for the Advancement of Science; the Academy of Science of South Africa; die Suid-Afrikaanse Akademie vir Wetenskap en Kuns; the World Academy of Sciences; and gold medals from Wellcome. He has been President of the Royal Society of South Africa (1987–1988) and of the Academy of Science of South Africa (1998–2004). He is the recipient of three honorary doctorates, the most recent from Stellenbosch University in 2013, and he has also been awarded the President's Order of Mapungubwe in Silver.

Some academics at universities actively seek executive leadership positions, others spurn them, and some have the role thrust upon them.[1]

Scholarly leadership in the most general sense is exercised within a discipline (as full professors or heads of department), either as a highly regarded individual scholar or as someone who assembles and builds a strong group of teachers, researchers and students which collectively acquires a good reputation. Such activity is generally so intellectually and emotionally satisfying that few participants imagine that anything better is available, except perhaps in another institution with even more opportunities to ply one's craft in generally the same way. The handful of apparently 'outlier' academics who aspire to, and occupy, posts which mainly carry executive or managerial responsibilities for systemic academic functions (vice-chancellors, rectors or their deputies, or executive deans) are widely regarded within academe with a mixture of pity and apprehension as fallen people who have sold their souls for the scholarly equivalent of a mess of pottage. For many years, I shared this view of the 'bosses' of the two South African institutions where I worked.

The reflections which follow arise from my realisation, through actual experience, that it is indeed possible to retain a basically scholarly orientation while holding full-time executive academic responsibility in a university. This means continuing to give primacy to the set of values which define academe, that is, to be empirical and coherent in addressing problems of institutional management, to be original and creative as far as possible, and to continue to learn new things about what one is doing and about the world in general. I am not saying that one will necessarily always be successful in fulfilling these aspirations in every assignment within one's bailiwick, but these are the principles which seem most appropriate to guide what one does within the constraints of every situation.

The most important implication of this approach is that simply reacting ad hoc to every challenge arising in an executive job cannot possibly be enough to do justice to the responsibility one holds, even though many members of the academic community tend to be appreciative of this style of leadership as most compatible with their desired comfort levels. ("Rule only when rule is directly needed, otherwise stay out of the way"). This is, of course, not the approach within a discipline

---

1   This echoes the line that Shakespeare has Malvolio read in *Twelfth Night*: "Some are born great, some achieve greatness, and some have greatness thrust upon them."

of a serious scholar who creatively seeks to open up original ways of seeing and thinking about the world. It is not in the nature of true scholarship to accept things as they appear to be, or to leave unexplored the underlying phenomena behind each challenge. Sticking to the broad scholarly modus operandi when becoming an executive academic leader leads to a significant degree of pro-activism in support of a medium- or long-term change perspective, with the accompanying risk of turbulence, but I firmly believe that this is what leadership, specifically in academe, is all about. There may be humiliating failures: so be it. That also happens in the scholarly life of teaching and research, but the idea is to score a reasonably high percentage of successes, and to let history judge.

Accepting a portfolio in an institutional leadership team is supposed (according to some modern ideas of management) to involve approaching the set of assigned responsibilities as a contract-long challenge to master detail (including getting to know all the individuals who will be needed as partners and allies), adopting a vision of what would be the most desirable set of outcomes, and fashioning and implementing a comprehensive plan of action over time. This may be possible for people who move to a university executive post from the same kind of appointment elsewhere; it is unlikely to work for a first-time appointee. Giving oneself the time to settle in, one can take a fresh look at established practice, learn to engage with experienced administrative staff, and begin to establish the necessary evidence base for action and reform. In doing this, one also has to be aware that the internal and external operating environment may change, impacting on one's thinking, often necessitating revised approaches, and prompting occasional tactical retreats.

I have known some academics who entered executive management in order to opt out of the scholarly rat race and work comfortably from 9am to 5pm with an improved salary, taking on board the need to weather an occasional crisis or two. Freed from teaching (preparing lectures and endless marking) as well as research (reading hundreds of papers, mostly better than your own, applying for grants and competing for graduate students), life should now settle into a comfortable round of committee meetings, ritual attendances at functions, and ordering administrative staff about. Those executive leaders who are worth their salt, by contrast, work harder than they ever did as academics, since their overall task of improving an institution in significant and lasting ways is even more demanding than the undoubtedly challenging, but comparatively micro-level, sphere of diligent general academic activity in one discipline.

The key to the hard work required of effective university leaders is the notion of needing a proper vertical understanding of issues and action areas in order to develop an approach to them that is likely to survive the continual consultations and debates of academic decision-making. The easiest way to gain at least part of this understanding, the generic part, is by direct previous experience up the ladder of university functioning, from junior to senior ranks. It is helpful if this is gained in institutions other than the present one. This person-specific orientation is by no means sufficient and must be broadened, raised and amplified to the systemic (and currently applicable) level by careful investigation, as well as a much more thorough and focused examination, at all levels, of matters pertaining to any given issue. Proposals one puts forward must be based on available evidence, both pro and con, and must be argued as tightly as one would do in a scholarly or scientific paper. Information gathering should never be confined to documents, but should be enriched and contextualised by site visits, personal interviews, and comparisons with other similar situations. All this takes time and effort, but one's effectiveness as a leader is greatly enhanced, and the likelihood of embarrassing failures and exposures lessened.

Creativity, in the sense of being good at creating new ways of looking at things, of evolving new conceptual frameworks, of finding new solutions, or of building up new organisations, is a rare quality in scholars and even rarer in university executives.[2] It is closely related to, but not the same as originality, which amounts to having the knack of finding things out (aspects of human behaviour or natural scientific phenomena) before others do. Critically, creativity also consists of having the capacity and patience to try out new things in a systematic manner. Creative people ask (usually not aloud) more "Why do we do things this way?" questions than other people, because they are constantly seeking to cut through the thick congelation of traditional thinking or practice, and wonder if alternatives are feasible and practicable. As in the case of proactivist leaders already mentioned, creative leaders are associated with turbulent working environments.

The path before, in brief

In my early years, in a rural setting in the 'old South Africa', I was always taken by surprise at the outcomes of each step in my career. I mention

---

2   Gevers, W. (1978) 'Personality, creativity and achievement in science' at the University of Cape Town (UCT) inaugural lectures, New Series, p.55.

this because (as will become clear) the inherent unpredictability of outcomes is extremely relevant to the exercise of leadership in academe.

My father was a teacher, one of six children of an immigrant German missionary, with a doctorate in Education History from Goettingen (his thesis dealt with the education of black children in South Africa at German mission schools), and a massive bookcase covering an entire wall of his bedroom. I was fourth oldest of five siblings, and sampled the book treasures voraciously from the age of ten, with striking catholicity in my taste. I was also given to much exercise of the imagination, ample time for which was made possible by the interaction between a weak respiratory system and an endlessly drizzle-soaked environment in the furthest south-east corner of what is now Mpumalanga. I sought at school to satisfy my own curiosity, rather than to please my some-what variably qualified and dedicated teachers, always maintaining more or less the same good level in all my subjects, unable to decide which was the most, and which the least, interesting.

After considering music, architecture, and law, in that order, I settled down (apprehensively) to six years of rigidly specified undergraduate study in medicine at the University of Cape Town (UCT). While dili-gently meeting the requirements of good passes in the many different subjects, I did not challenge but rather received knowledge as it came to me in books and lectures. This was because my main intellectual pastimes were actually to read books (poetry, history, philosophy) in the main university library, listen to records in the music library, dilettantishly write poetry, paint with watercolours and play the piano. I edited a number of student publications, including the student research journal, *Inyanga*, and the university Rag magazine, *Sax Appeal*. I knew that a number of fellow-students were delving much more deeply than I was into the original scientific literature underlying each discipline, and that some were equipping themselves with better high-level practical skills. Avoiding further clinical training after graduation, having discovered that my tendency to foretell every imaginable com-plication, in every patient I had to look after, made life too stressful, I used the award of a Rhodes Scholarship to become a biochemist with an honours degree and a doctorate from the University of Oxford, supervised by a man who had won a Nobel Prize 13 years before and was known, even to schoolchildren, as the discoverer of the Krebs Cycle. I had also been enriched by a wife and two children.

During a productive postdoctoral period with an equally famous Nobelist in New York, I discovered not only a passion for empirical enquiry that I didn't know existed, but also identified the ingredients of effective research groups and the kinds of leadership that draw the best out of talented people. I undertook spells of teaching at both Oxford and Rockefeller universities, and found it immensely satisfying.

Returning to South Africa after eight years abroad, I turned a research chair at Stellenbosch University's Medical School into a new teaching department built around a flourishing research programme in a newly-constructed building, burnt the midnight oil to develop a teaching approach that was rigorous and inspirational at both undergraduate and postgraduate levels, and enjoyed my first experience of concerted curriculum reform across an entire faculty. I returned to UCT in 1978 to a similar situation, but with increased opportunities for creating new approaches to teaching (including devising a new multidepartmental, integrative course for medical students called Human Biology, setting up a cooperative system of modular honours courses in medical sciences, and achieving outreach through the College of Medicine to specialist training nationwide.) The birth of an entirely new multidisciplinary programme in sports science was also facilitated, later finding expression in an internationally recognised, off-campus institute devoted to this field. These activities whetted my appetite for academic innovation.

First encounters with the institutional centre

My first experience of a more central role in the University was when I was appointed, out of the blue, to a Senate committee, namely the Library Committee, and, more than that, to be its Chair. I hesitated before accepting, as I feared getting drawn into activity outside my consuming interest in teaching and research in my broad discipline of medical science. However, I thought the library was sufficiently close to my preoccupations, since the library service was crucial to what we were doing. At the starting time of my first committee meeting of 2pm, I discovered a crowd of over 40 assorted academics and library staff filling the largest available meeting room in the University, all expecting to go through an overlong agenda until evening, and puzzled to be presided over by a completely unknown fellow from the medical school. All my instincts soon rebelled against what I concluded was a monumental time-wasting exercise, as library policy was more or less set in stone and nothing ever changed, from year to year, decade to decade. Even though it would have been less disruptive to my own academic life to have done nothing other than to attend the prescribed minimum of four meetings a year, I began instinctively to contemplate drastic reform of the committee and its operations.

The arrival of a new, like-minded University Librarian provided the stimulus to effect a complete overhaul of the Library Committee, contracting it to nine members, drafting new terms of reference, and linking it to newly created library subcommittees in each of the nine faculties. The Library's internal matters were henceforth to be left to its executive management. The acquisition policy for books was reconsidered by a commission chaired by a professor of librarianship, which, controversially, but I believe correctly, recommended a change from a system based on a complex formula involving internal statistical drivers and weightings, to one termed 'collection development'. This sought to make acquisitions that reflected the largest affordable fraction of the best of the scholarly books that were published each year in the broad domains covered by the University's faculties. The reform went through, despite much grumbling, because it was difficult to fault a policy that was promoted on rational grounds by the powerful alliance of expertise we had fashioned. I must confess that the actual implementation of the new acquisition system proved very troublesome, mainly because of a failure of nerve on the part of the Library in the face of the many people who hadn't ever noticed that there was a new policy and who kept reverting to the practices of the old system. Eventually, my successors as chairs of the Library Committee quietly returned the acquisition policy to something resembling its previous activity-reflecting formula model. I noted that the sky didn't fall, but concluded that lasting, followed-through change would require a different university governance model (see below).

It was to be one of the too many examples in my reformist career where the forces of habit and inertia overcame the momentum of change and restored the status quo. I became uncertain of my aptitude for institutional change management and returned to my happy departmental academic life.

Into the deep end

Despite this negative experience, I did agree, with reluctance and apprehension, to act as leave replacement for a number of deputy vice-chancellors (DVCs) between 1990 and 1991, rotating through different portfolio areas. I was thrown into the deep end by having to chair the executive committee of the Senate, comprising mostly deans and Executive Officers, in my second week of acting service. I ended my first meeting with a brave face but completely drenched in anxiety-provoked sweat after four-and-a-half nightmarish hours.

The system of academic governance was entrenched, at the time, in well-established rules and practices that brooked little change, and this made for a useful and thorough immersion on my part in a highly structured and stable, committee-based decision-making model which could readily be controlled from above by the central executive under the Vice-Chancellor (VC). The latter, in turn, was very close to the Chairperson of the University Council, so that meetings of this august body were smooth and well prepared, with all surprises headed off beforehand. (Reportedly, the Secretary of the Council on one occasion completed drafting the minutes before the meeting was concluded). The smoothness of the operation was just as well, as the institution had to prepare for a sea of changes in the racial and class composition of the student body, which required steady hands and strong moral leadership. The only unsatisfactory feature of what was otherwise an exemplary administration, was that there was too little room for creativity or innovation, other than responsively to crisis.

Amongst the first matters practically forced on my attention, was my relationship with the deans of the ten faculties, which had been in existence longer than anybody could remember. I was aware from my own faculty that the prevailing model of deanship appointment was a bottom-up process in which the faculty 'barons' pushed forward somebody from amongst their lesser ranks who they thought would be least likely to 'rock the boat', that is, who would 'comfortably warm the seat', represent the 'least loss to the academic effort' and be a 'staunch defender of the status quo' (all the terms in inverted commas in the above text are, of course, mine, not theirs, but the reader will readily understand). I understood the context, as I had been such a 'baron' myself.

The easiest way to run my portfolio was to fall in with the deans and their backers, to seek popularity as a 'good guy on the executive with whom one can work'. This was fine, and I complied until I understood my job better. However, the difficulties of managing the recurrent University budget crises, requiring extensive savings from the faculties as well as the central administration, brought out a crucial weakness of the 'weak dean' model of governance. On every occasion, the savings had to be forced on the deans and their faculties, mainly as an unstrategic and unwise freezing of all vacant posts, irrespective of the consequences for function and the opportunities of beneficial change. After the budget crisis, the blocked posts were simply restored to the same departments which had had to do without them, and life went on for two to three years until the next debacle.

At that time, the VC wisely chaired, with great care, every selection committee for every professorship in every faculty. Such posts were usually linked to departmental headships, and were critical investments for the University, since the impact of an excellent appointee was amplified over a long period of time through its positive effects on the department concerned. On the rare occasions when the VC couldn't do the job, a DVC had to stand in for him, and so my long career as a selection committee chair began, in fits and starts, in this phase. It is not often that one's judgement and chairing skills are as openly tested as in the start-up period of a new chair of such a committee. I also became convinced that the University's future largely depended on the Chair's interventions.

It took a certain amount of courage to stand up during selection committee meetings to the walls of support for candidates who suited faculty members' purposes more than they promised lively intellectual returns to the institution as a whole. I was threatened with impeachment on one occasion, when I found myself as one of a handful who stoutly defended appointing a 30-year-old bright spark, fresh from a groundbreaking doctorate at the University of Oxford, who was a black South African to boot, against an array of strongly-held opinion that a journeyman specialist from a neighbouring medical school represented a sounder choice. I retreated, and they won; the successful appointee left the University and emigrated not long afterwards.

Exercising power in academe

I soon discovered that a key question was that of how power was exercised in the academic sphere. When I assumed the office of DVC, heads of department, usually also appointed simultaneously with unique tenured professorships in the discipline concerned, wielded an extraordinary degree of control over their staff and departmental activities, on an open-ended basis, till death or retirement. This was a major contributing factor to the weak-dean faculty model mentioned earlier. Three developments brought about a radical change in this situation during my 12 years in office. First was the introduction of rotation into headships at periodic intervals, resulting typically in a weak-head model where the job was done reluctantly and with a minimum of mainly administratively focused effort. Second was the rapid evolution of a pervasive ad hominem promotion system by means of which the number of people holding full professorships increased dramatically, effectively disconnecting headships from professorships. The final development was the conversion of deanships into contract executive positions, centralising faculty power, realised through a distributed faculty committee system that further constrained the powers of individual heads of department.

I twice had the experience of setting up a new department, in different institutions. That was made possible only by the concentration of final decision-making power in my hands. This meant strategising and planning over a clear horizon of time, while taking full responsibility for success or failure. In both cases, I learnt that something approaching a democratic form of governance could be achieved by a highly consultative approach, but it was always helpful that one could break opinion deadlocks by simply deciding one way or the other. The same can be said for the executive deans who inherited the final decision-making prerogative in the newer model of faculty governance. Rotating headships are a formula for stasis unless someone comes into office and is given enough rope to create something new without hanging himself or herself. My impression was that only rarely was there much change during the tenure of a temporary headship. I fully concede that permanent headships can be, and frequently have been, disastrous if the wrong persons are appointed, so perhaps what one wins from creativity in some cases one loses by poor leadership in others. Perhaps a probationary period before a long-term headship is confirmed would be the right answer.

Widespread ad hominem promotions have, for obvious reasons, been very popular, and have permitted institutions to retain talented staff that in previous eras might have migrated to other universities or countries. Promotions incentivise each staff member to project a meritocratic trajectory that can go right to the top. They provide candidates for headship in the rotating system, and are particularly good for building large research teams. The systemic drawback is that the academic marketplace has been seriously impaired by the comfort zones established by the availability of such opportunities in each institution. This has meant that much potential creativity has been lost as academics are no longer inclined to 'seek the sun in new settings', as was the case, for example, when the outstanding Scottish scholar–leaders in the 19th and early 20th centuries emigrated to take up permanent chairs in Australia and South Africa because their progress to chairs was blocked in their home country. My belief is that ad hominem promotions should be scaled down, or otherwise modified, in order to allow a fuller degree of mobility to be restored to the academic market-place and so help build a system of diverse but strong institutions.

University (Pty) Ltd

The third major change, that of executive deans, has been part of the corporatisation of university management by turning councils into boards of directors, VCs into chief executive officers (CEOs), and deans into something approximating production managers, in addition to turning students into customers or clients, and staff into that terrible entity, human resources. Mission statements and strategic plans have become key instruments for governance, and the language of the factory has become the stuff of its discourse. Implementation of information technology and business software packages is the expensive and game-changing, but also highly problematic, handmaiden of such a transition.

I must record a mea culpa for my own role in going along with such a transformation of institutional governance, which I did mainly in order to address the real issue of academic stasis I had repeatedly identified as the key problem standing in the way of dynamism and creative change for the University. The tension between my true aspiration and the trappings of the corporate model became so great that I actually burst into uncontrollable tears during a meeting of university executives aimed at agreeing on the supposedly final version of the Strategic Plan of the University. I had painfully overseen it to its 14th iteration, only to hear a languid analysis by a relatively outsider participant that suggested we had a bad product and should start again from the very beginning. Not a good moment, but a necessary learning experience.

What I sought from changes in university governance was not to turn the University into a company, but to construct a vibrant system in which new ideas coming from creative individuals, be they 'robber baron', heads of department, visionary deans, reformist DVCs, or whoever, would be taken seriously, debated vigorously by all who could contribute, and implemented with adequate resource allocation. To illustrate what I mean, I can briefly describe the memorable occasion, under the pre-corporate dispensation, when a proposal from a special planning group, which included me, for a United States-style liberal arts-focused undergraduate college (based at the embarrassingly underutilised original and still substantial downtown UCT campus at Hiddingh Hall) was not discussed at a Senate meeting because an earlier item on parking policies had taken up all the meeting time. A second example came up during the first audit conducted under the auspices of the association of vice-chancellors, which revealed that very few proposals that had gone through the Senate had ever been turned down, or even modified, as a result of a general debate on their merits. The old-style role of the Senate was to allow each faculty to decide what it wanted, and tacitly to agree never to oppose proposals brought forward by other faculties. One of the most amusing features of the old-style Senate meetings was the huge amount of paper that went into the printed agendas, which resulted in a loud whirring sound dominating meetings as attendees tried frantically to keep up with the business being transacted with their assumed consent.

I do not regret the big governance changes at UCT in respect of which I played a significant role and assisted a dynamic VC to bring about:

the institution was irreversibly changed and has gone from strength to strength, at least partly, I hope, because of these changes. I attribute this to the fact that the corporatisation process was never allowed to proceed to completion, for example, in the extreme case, by appointing a top businesswoman as VC! In fact, the deans of the new system have in the main been a much stronger set of scholars and leaders than their predecessors, and they, in turn, have sought to appoint stronger heads of academic departments, who have appointed stronger and more research-active staff members. The executive directors of service departments have also been appointed more competitively and have, therefore, been much stronger too, although, on the negative side, this has been accompanied by a proliferation of administrative staff. Over-all, a more vital, more capable and generally more change-friendly climate was in fact achieved.

The body of academe

My greatest day-to-day satisfaction in the DVC job was the enriching contact with large numbers of individual scholars across the University that was made possible by my frenetic involvement in the things they thought were important, such as the desired recruitment from outside of star academics, conversely the retention of somebody who might be lost, academic planning, space issues, inaugural lectures, new books, and the like. I made lasting friends as well as enemies, but my respect for both categories of people inured me to anger or resentment. At the level of the individual scholar, I felt nothing but a sense of great privilege just knowing so many of them.

My special favourites were the academics in the creative arts. In my interactions in this domain, I chaired a simultaneous selection process for three new piano teachers, with master classes thrown in as bonselas into the usual mix of interviews and hard-argued debate. I posed with a few other hand-picked colleagues (one of them John M. Coetzee) as a 12th-century *geistliche* for a photographic essay on the essence of spirituality. I routinely attended the student plays in the University theatres, marvelling at their maturity and freshness. I oversaw a funding proposal for a United States of America (USA) foundation to upscale the opera training programme in order to cope with a large influx of black opera students with well-nigh miraculous talent. A little further from my own interests, the ballet and dance students also had to be seen to be believed. All in all, I am hoping that the unexpected reality of reincarnation would find me amongst these supremely gifted people.

My other virtually enforced focus, bearing in mind my own career trajectory in medical science, was the eternally complicated world of the Faculty of Medicine, along with its twin-like partners, the academic hospitals under the provincial health department. My period as DVC was accompanied by endless crises in the health services. These were partly brought about by a near-catastrophic and ideologically driven service reorganisation, which was based on a zero-sum notion of rebalancing in favour of primary and secondary care at the expense of the tertiary and quaternary levels. It was also a result of a wrong-headed belief that the domain of service (the responsibility of the province) and that of education, training and research (the University's role) could be completely separated, and that they could be planned and funded in two parallel systems that totally disregarded each other's priorities and operational modes. The province tried at one stage to reverse the historical circumstance, in its day also driven by ideology, that two large-scale health science faculties were placed within 20 kilometres of each other, by now unaffordably so. This is not the place to relate the history of the resulting conflicts, which in time assumed the gravity of those in Northern Ireland, Palestine/Israel and Cyprus. Suffice it to say that most of the grey hairs on my head were certainly occasioned by my necessary involvement in this protracted tussle. After my retirement in 2002, I returned to this faculty to establish a major research institute (see below).

Raising money to pay for it all

I was directly concerned with fundraising three times during my long stint as DVC. The first early one was a cautionary experience of assisting the VC in a broad 'education for the future' campaign. I learnt the ropes, so to speak, and discovered the hard grind that fundraising constitutes in South Africa. Nobody ever seemed to want to give to the whole institution; each donor was prepared to support only a pet project, which was usually not a priority for the University.

The second fundraising adventure was the massive so-called 'upper-campus project' years later, when I found myself (now as senior DVC) at the centre of a major tug of war between a new VC and large parts of the establishment that had called the shots in the previous regime. This concerned the reversal of an already-processed decision to use a substantial donation for a single, new academic building, in favour of a much larger and more strategic enterprise, requiring much more money, to revamp large elements of the main upper campus, namely the Library, student services, several faculty headquarters, and several other buildings. The fundraising campaign was well organised but brutal in its demands on all of us. I had to ensure that key disaffected people were won over to the new project, that the architects did not scale up their visions to well above the maximum budget (I was told I had been called a thug by the chief architect), and that downstream consequences of all the changes were planned and managed.

The third fundraising task was left almost entirely to me to drive after my retirement as DVC in 2002 – trying to house a large research institute in a set of run-down, period buildings on the old medical school campus. I could not have achieved the set target if it had not been for the tough school of my earlier experiences in this field.

How hard do these guys really work?

My instinct for seeking solutions to problems by looking under the surface of the phenomena led me to investigate the manner in which posts were allocated to departments and faculties. It turned out that the decisions of the Central Staffing Committee were based on a combination of factors, chief of which were the size of the establishment heretofore, the loudness of the requester's voice, and the immediate persuasiveness of the 'sob story' about staff overwork. There was no remotely reliable measuring instrument for staff workloads in comparable circumstances in different departments or faculties, and no way to link individual applications to strategic objectives or curriculum reforms.

With the enthusiastic help of the Central Staffing Officer, who had had her fill of the aforementioned inchoate system, I assumed the chairing of the Central Staffing Committee and began, with misgivings but in desperation, to devise a generally applicable teaching portfolio in which each academic staff member could record all teaching commitments, at all levels of instruction or supervision (new or repeat courses), in scheduled hours of lectures, seminars, tutorials and practicals per week (with class sizes in each case), plus estimates of time spent on consultations, setting and marking of tests and examinations, and *new* preparation work. The teething problems in this project were indeed formidable. It was quickly revealed that the biggest and mostly inexplicable variations were in unstructured activities such as preparation and marking, where indeed norms could only be set with great difficulty because people do vary greatly in the trouble and time they take with these tasks, depending on temperament and the skills levels they have attained. Despite this, the staff teaching portfolios did provide a kind of 'under oath' written statement which could be tested with heads of department and other colleagues in a particular community of practice. When the teaching profile system began to reach Senate and faculty boards for consideration and adoption, the reactions were divided into those that were contemptuous (the majority), and those few who were sceptical but constructive. The best of these were efforts to revise or improve the logic of the portfolios, and to help us to make them more acceptable and embedded in the culture of the faculty concerned.

The whole sorry story of staff workload determination was suddenly cut short when the University, as one of the implementation steps of the Academic Planning Framework (see below), adopted a new faculty structure and delegated resource allocation, especially for staff, to executive deans. The Central Staffing Committee was no more, and, with it, ended my effort to provide a valid measuring instrument for the huge long-term investment made by the institution when any post was released and filled for tenure, for up to 40 years in many cases.

Collegial leadership

I have mentioned elsewhere that the unavoidable overlaps between DVC portfolios may have caused friction from time to time, but were more likely to be the crucibles of new thinking in key areas of the University. I enjoyed interacting with my fellow DVCs on matters of shared responsibility and usually agreed on a division of labour if this was appropriate. My intense personal interest in research, my close involvement with deans, my responsibility for postgraduate study, and my belief that teaching and research were inextricably linked, meant that this was an area where I would have to work closely with my colleague, the DVC for Research and Innovation.

Near the end of my terms as DVC, the Academic Planning Committee set up a task group, which I chaired, to make proposals for systemic reform of the way in which postgraduate studies were organised at UCT. We worked hard and well, producing a report that, inter alia recommended the establishment of a Centre for Postgraduate Studies in a prime upper-campus location that would provide a home for all services required by research students (such as financial aid, housing, study visas, and the like); a central board for graduate studies and committees in each faculty set up for this purpose; the conversion of the narrowly focused Scholarships Committee into a much broader postgraduate funding committee; the introduction of memoranda of understanding between doctoral students and their supervisors; attention to safety on campus after hours; and a requirement for a personal progress portfolio to be maintained by each doctoral student in order to encourage them to take full responsibility for their own trajectory towards degree completion. Most of these recommendations were implemented in the following years, although my pet idea of the portfolio never caught on, which I still think was a pity.

One of my colleagues did superb work on similar lines to enhance the studies of both undergraduate and postgraduate international students at UCT, with lasting benefits. Again, the work was conducted across the DVC portfolio lines, but somebody had to conceive the plan and carry it through, with help from others as required. Such activities were amongst the most gratifying I experienced in my time as DVC, and they exemplify the notion of applying a scholarly approach, with scholarly values, to leadership challenges in academe.

My substantive appointment with responsibility for academic affairs and planning took me in due course through hectic tugs of war with the student leadership on academic readmission issues, seeking to preserve, through thick and thin, the basic principle of demonstrable academic potential as the determining yardstick. Battles were often lost, but the war was won, so to speak, and readmission review processes were eased into place that kept the peace on the campus for half a decade or more. One must emphasise here that achieving this outcome required close teamwork between the DVC for Student Affairs and me, as well as a real effort to get to know the student leadership and to meet it halfway.

The prominence of the readmission issue in this period of transformation of the student body, and my suspicion that a key source of trouble for the students in the contested borderline group was the poor alignment between their problematic schooling and the structure of university study, made me realise just how necessary it was to initiate reform of outdated curriculum models. I began to take the work undertaken by the dedicated staff of the Academic Development Programme (ADP) more and more seriously, as they had the greatest insight into the precise difficulties posed by curricula used by the faculties, not only for students coming from disadvantaged schools, but also for those drawn from the traditional catchments.

Putting hands into a hive full of angry bees

My intense involvement in the work of the National Commission on Higher Education (NCHE), and my interest in whole-qualification standards, caused me in 1995 to propose a new Academic Planning Framework' (APF) for UCT. The most controversial part of the document had to do with a major reshaping of the faculty substructure and organisational model, to be investigated in depth by a special commission charged with recommending an optimal distribution of departments in the faculties, and a changed conception of the roles of deans.

The real core idea in the APF, however, was to require departments, faculties and Senate to move from the local, traditional model of curricula primarily based on the specification of *degree structure* (minimum numbers of courses at different levels, each examined independently and individually to a minimum achievement level), to one based on the specification of *degree purpose* (planned combinations of core and optional supplementary or complementary courses, at different levels, with examination outcomes determined by minimum achievement of the relevant degree purpose).

I was particularly keen on the elaboration of many new, so-called service courses by means of which the more 'fundamental' faculties, such as those in the humanities, social and natural sciences, could cooperatively construct entirely new amalgams of relevant parts of different disciplines to furnish the students of the more professional or applied faculties, such as commerce, engineering and medicine, with mind-broadening contextualisations of their narrow preoccupations. A useful by-product would be the rational enlargement of the teaching workloads of small, but excellent, fundamental departments under threat of closure or loss of staff positions because of decreasing numbers of their own mainstream students.

The word that became 'code-speak' for the curriculum component of the APF was 'programme', intended to denote the purposes of particular degree variants that were newly curriculated in terms (at the different year-levels) of compulsory core courses, sets of optional cognate or support courses, and further choices designed to help bring about the achievement by most, if possible all, students enrolled for the particular degree variant concerned. This was not in itself at all original, plentiful examples in the general studies areas being available at much-admired universities such as Oxford in the United Kingdom (UK) and Princeton in the USA. The degree programme at Oxford called Philosophy, Politics and Economics (PPE) became the prototype to illustrate the nature of the beast, as it were, to those (and there were many) who refused to believe that anything other than the conventional, local degree model had ever existed anywhere.

It became necessary to draw attention, over and over, to the curious fact that several faculties at the University were accustomed constantly to mull over the optimal design of their curricula, and had decades ago brought forward the concept of 'degree purpose driving degree structure' as proposed for the whole institution by the APF. Admittedly, these were the professional faculties such as medicine and engineering, with professional councils breathing down their necks. The departure in the APF at UCT was that the general-studies faculties should also reflect on the purposes of their degrees, and examine whether their current 'rules and structure' model was best for students in a South

African university, at this time. In this connection, one could note the intense debates at the Ivy League institutions in the USA on the core curricula of their liberal arts degrees.

There isn't space here for a full description of the 'APF wars' that eventually erupted at UCT after the distinctly underdebated programme approach to the general undergraduate degrees was adopted, in rapid succession, by the Academic Planning Committee, Senate and Council. I was in constant touch with somewhat frantic faculty committees charged with reorganising their particular structure- and rule-determined degrees into sets of designed-for-purpose degree programmes. As each faculty succeeded, with much grumbling from rebellious factions, in more or less shoehorning everything they offered into an (equally more or less) generally accepted set of such programmes, the realisation dawned on all concerned that the transition from the previous multiyear system to a very different, new multiyear system would entail considerable administrative complexity and much confusion amongst staff, students and administrators, unless it was very well handled. Despite this, the momentum of the sea change that seemed to be happening carried it through to general implementation in a new academic year, with extra-thick faculty handbooks symbolising the situation.

Into this highly charged atmosphere came an almost irrelevant intrusion by a newly appointed, high-profile foreign scholar, brought up in the USA liberal arts undergraduate system of small-group, personally and highly autonomously taught courses, who objected strongly to the locally prevalent model of team-based course design and delivery. This issue became conflated with the programme concept of degree studies, with which it was, strictly speaking, not necessarily in conflict, but the episode brought the UCT curriculum issue into the national media, and became the trigger for a tacit consensus amongst most members of the UCT academic community that the programme system should be quietly dismantled, from below so to speak, retaining only those (few) constructs which had proved successful in attracting students and which have survived and, in fact, prospered to this day. These included structured degrees in PPE in both the Humanities and Commerce faculties, and Film and Media Studies in the Faculty of Humanities.

Hands in a bigger national hive, with more (and even angrier) bees

At this point I must pause my account of the APF debacle at UCT to go back in time to another related epic into which I found myself drawn, against my better judgement, persuaded by the idea that the core issue of curriculum might be approached more successfully from another, more systemic, direction.

My proposals for the National Qualifications Framework (NQF) in higher education for the NCHE led to my being appointed as the (regrettably only) representative of all public universities on the newly constituted South African Qualifications Authority (SAQA) in 1996. This, in turn, caused me to become active in the Education Committee of the South African Universities Vice-Chancellors' Association (SAUVCA), of which I was for two years the Acting Chairperson.

At the time, the main imperative was to protect higher education from serious, perhaps irretrievable, damage likely to arise from the ideology-driven SAQA notion of 'unit standards' as a one-size-fits-all approach towards the entire educational system. I was convinced that university qualifications could only be part of a single framework of all educational qualifications if the standards to be adopted were those of whole qualifications, rather than those of a virtual universe of variably constituent units of learning and training. It seemed feasible to adapt the SAQA approach of national standards-setting bodies in this way, and simultaneously to bring about a systemic rethink on the purpose and structure of the most widely offered generic degrees. From my minority-of-one position on the SAQA board, I offered a way forward (mandated by SAUVCA) that, after much heated debate, was adopted by the Authority for the development of the NQF within the higher education subsector.

The acceptance of a whole-qualifications approach for higher educa-tion came with the challenge that I now had to provide the necessary leadership for an optimal system logic and process. This was awkward, as the universities had strongly opposed the inclusion of higher education in the NQF, and the general degree of suspicion of what was happening at SAQA was intense.

It was decided that SAUVCA's Education Committee should be the driver of a number of selected standards-generating bodies (SGBs) to pilot the application of NQF principles to the most commonly offered bachelor's degrees. With able assistance from within the SAUVCA office, five such SGBs were set up, with representation from across the university system, respectively taking on the BA/BSocSci, BSc, BCom, BSc Engineering and LLB degrees. The work was slow because it was unfamiliar, and participants were variously uncertain of their actual mandate, of the likelihood that anything would ever come of the exercise, and of the possibility of damage to their reputations. In the end, some of the products of this SGB work were placed before the SAQA board, but momentum was lost as the focus of this body shifted to another, much more ambitious, exercise, namely an attempt to get every existing higher education qualification approved and registered in an NQF-aligned form, a kind of concerted, fast-track conversion that required massive effort from every institution. The SAUVCA team, under my direction, drafted a guidebook to aid the task of writing all the qualification descriptions in what had by now become known (usually derisively) as 'SAQA-speak'.

My role in these increasingly intrusive NQF-related interventions into university administration was becoming problematic for me, as many university leaders, and certainly most of their more vocal staff, believed we should never have 'supped with the devil' at all. Most difficult was the fact that my own institutional leadership was perhaps the most opposed of all to having any dealings with SAQA, and the uneven course of APF implementation within UCT made the matter even more complicated for me. The belief, both at UCT and in the other institutions represented within SAUVCA, had been quite strong up to this point that I was a kind of Horatio at the bridge, heroically defending the system, and not letting it become affected by the madness of the NQF. The truth was that I was, in fact, a double agent arising from my above-mentioned interest in curriculum reform, and my hope that the university system might respond to the threat of damage from SAQA, and its inappropriate ideas concerning higher education, by agreeing to necessary reform from within of the curriculum system in order to improve the educational experience of all students, and especially those disadvantaged by poor school preparation.

The lessons of the APF debacle at UCT were many. The support one might have expected from those faculties long accustomed to collective mulling over curricula, was not forthcoming. Despite the well-worn notion of universities being best governed in their academic sphere by senates with membership drawn from all faculties, few senators ever venture forth, singly or in groups, to subject to scrutiny the practices and core beliefs of faculties other than their own.

Another lesson was that a national process will only rarely affect the thinking of a particular institution in a significant way. I thought the threat of really unacceptable change forced from above might move the academics to defending their existing turf from internally driven reform initiatives and to budge from their entrenched positions, but they were mostly unaware of the storm clouds or considered them as only affecting other institutions, not theirs.

Out of the rhetoric and myth-making of the APF wars at UCT came the pervasive belief in the humanities faculties (or similar) at South African universities that all the trouble had been caused by rampant 'managerialism' on the part of university leaders who knew nothing, or too little at best, about 'true' scholarship and the eternal verities of how young people are best taught to think, reflect, write, and lead in society. I rest my case that this was in fact not so, not any part of it.[3]

My university, right or wrong?

One of the most intriguing aspects of institutional leadership is the question of the boundaries of one's loyalty. Many regard the appropriate attitude as 'my university, right or wrong', in which losses or failings of sister institutions are regarded with schadenfreude as a plus-for-self in a zero-sum game. My preference was for an approach that saw one's own institution as needing to be as strong as possible, and leading the way as far as it could, whenever it could, in a broader framework of successful partnerships and constructive rivalry that comprised a system which needed to move forward as a whole for the good of society and the economy.

My consequent enthusiasm for inter-institutional cooperation led me to initiate a Vice-Rectors' Group (VRG) among five higher education institutions in the Western Cape.[4] I convened dinner workshops which were held in rotation at the participating institutions, and which soon established the ground rules of cooperation. These explicitly excluded formal sharing of academic teaching programmes but instead concentrated on mutual strengthening of support services and joint involvement in externally directed outreach activities.

The VRG later became the legally constituted Western Cape Tertiary Institutions Trust, which, in turn, transmuted into the Adamastor Trust, with a near full-time executive officer, its own offices successively at various locations in Cape Town, and an operating budget provided annually, on the basis of an agreed formula, by the participating institutions. The chairing of the Trust became based on a two-yearly rotation between the designated vice-rectors or DVCs, and a greater degree of accountability to, and integration of policy with, each home institution was now required. My own role began to lessen as my duties as Senior DVC of UCT expanded dramatically from late 1996 onwards.

The first of several successes of the VRG was the formation of the Cape Library Consortium (CALICO), a consortia library system largely funded by the A.W. Mellon Foundation in the USA. The initial idea

---

3 Gevers, W. (2003) 'The social sciences, the human genome and human nature' in *The South African Medical Journal*, 100, pp.354–356.
4 The term 'vice-rector' as opposed to 'deputy vice-chancellor' was then used in a majority of the three universities and two technikons in the group.

found favour with all of the chief librarians, with those from the historically disadvantaged institutions expressing the most enthusiasm. I chaired innumerable difficult meetings of the CALICO Steering Committee and oversaw the drafting of the proposals for funding from several USA foundations. Once funding was secured, with sympathetic but firm pressure from the funder for the meeting of deadlines, the project acquired such momentum that the system was soon in place. The momentum extended to other regions in the country with the formation of variably effective consortia and shared library systems in Gauteng, on the eastern seaboard and in the Eastern Cape.

I must leave it to others to chronicle the subsequent course of this innovative attempt to maximise the information resources available to staff and students of the five higher education institutions in the Western Cape. My impression is that the wind was taken out of its sails in the journals domain by the advent of bundled electronic subscriptions negotiated at national consortium level with publishers, and then purchased under licence by individual institutions for their own users only. Hard copies of books are another matter, and here the case for a consortia approach to purchasing, storing and lending remains strong, at least until e-books become the norm.

Another project of the regional higher education trust was an ambitious effort jointly to establish a major science museum or exploratorium in Cape Town. This initially took the form of a mobile (bus) laboratory with a range of hands-on exhibits and features, and got close enough to the realisation of a permanent public home for a complete set of plans to have been prepared by a prominent architect for the conversion of thousands of square metres of a historic building in central Cape Town into a world-class museum. A single person, unusually gifted in creating such institutions and raising money for them, anticipated the initiative by obtaining sponsorship for an impressive (but unfortunately not long-lived) science museum in an urban mall, with minimal involvement of the higher education institutions.

An ambitious attempt to establish a jointly run School of Public Health under the auspices of the Trust foundered on the twin rocks of vested interests and the intricacies of university funding mechanisms. All the higher education institutions at this time were expanding their activities in community and public health, and the very ethos of this domain cried out for cooperation and the pulling down of fences. Unfortunately, we failed to pull it off, even with the active involvement of some of the most influential personalities in the region (one later became a provincial premier while another was appointed director-general of a government department). I learnt from this painful episode that the original Trust decision to avoid fostering direct academic cooperation had been a wise one, since the dice one tried to throw were loaded heavily against this otherwise obviously advantageous notion. Fortunately, the core cooperative enterprise still exists and flourishes today as the Cape Higher Education Consortium (CHEC).

Building an institution from scratch: A new national science academy

Although not directly related to university leadership, an extramural activity that featured prominently in my life during my tenure as DVC was the establishment of a new, discipline-inclusive science academy for the newly democratised country, eventually launched in 1996 as the Academy of Science of South Africa (ASSAf). South Africa had two 100-year-old bodies claiming to be the national science academies of the country – the Royal Society of South Africa (RSSAf) and the Suid-Afrikaanse Akademie vir Wetenskap en Kuns (SAAWEK), but they were largely limited respectively to white English- and Afrikaans-speakers. I had been President of the RSSAf between 1987 and 1988 and agreed for the following two two-year terms also to be its General Secretary, in order to continue the rejuvenation of the society we had begun earlier.[5]

Discussions were initiated as early as 1991 under the Foundation for Research Development (FRD) between the RSSAf, SAAWEK and a black-led organisation called the Science and Engineering Academy of South Africa (SEASA) to draw up a plan for the formation of a new, inclusive national science academy that would be a potentially significant public entity in the new democratic nation. I became deeply involved in these sometimes turbulent interactions, ultimately being the main writer of both the plan for the formation of ASSAf and its draft constitution. We overcame considerable opposition to achieve the main distinguishing features of the new Academy, namely its inclusion of all scholarship that was empirical in nature (across the natural, medical, social/human, technological/engineering, economic and legal sciences), and its membership selection criteria based on a combination of excellence in scholarship and demonstrable service to society through that scholarship.

Most national academies style themselves as being 'academies of sciences', implying acceptance of the post-structuralist notion of disciplines existing on their own in the knowledge sphere. I fought hard to persuade the planning team to take the minority path of calling

---

5   Gevers, W. (1998) 'Royal Society of South Africa presidential lecture, 1989: The art of the insoluble' in *Transactions of the Royal Society of South Africa*, 47, pp.111–118.

the new body an 'academy of science', emphasising the commonality of evidence-based enquiry among all of the disciplines, explicitly endorsing the concept of 'consilience' developed by the American naturalist, E.O. Wilson. This choice was adumbrated in my Presidential Lecture in 2003, published subsequently in the *South African Journal of Science*.[6]

I became the second President of ASSAf for three terms from 1998 to 2004, overseeing the processes that led to its being granted a parliamentary statute in 2001 as the country's only body of this kind, recognised nationally and internationally. It was hard going initially, with much difficulty in getting council members to attend meetings, hostility from the pre-existing academy-type bodies (SAAWEK lost its notionally de facto preeminent position through the repeal of its statute as part of the ASSAf Act 67 of 2001), and suspicion from government itself, as well as some research councils, about the positioning of ASSAf as a newcomer in the science system.

The Academy was fortunate in entering the field without all the baggage of exclusive elitism that had been the hallmark of national science academies, and still was in many other African academies. Our core activity was to be the generation of evidence-based advice on questions of national importance, which was the new focus of the strongest national science academies worldwide. The previous idea of operating an academy as a 'club of science heroes' was neatly turned into using its demonstrable excellence across the disciplinary spectrum and relative freedom from agendas as the basis of impartial, multiperspective and ultimately transparent analysis of issues that otherwise would be examined and pronounced upon by paid consultants or government-appointed panels or commissions.

In principle, the Academy was positioned to be the vehicle through which the country's outstanding intellectuals could individually and collectively contribute to national development in the most appropriate and independent manner, using the basic approaches and methodologies that served them in their everyday work. This made the establishment of a working academy an exciting project for me, even though most of the developmental work was only done after I retired from my DVC post at UCT, in the years from 2004. It was a little sad to have to deal with resistance to the new academy from adherents of the bodies that had claimed the territory in the old South Africa, but the

---

6 Gevers, W. (2003) 'Academy of Science of South Africa presidential lecture 2003: "Science" or "sciences" – the difference one letter makes' in *South African Journal of Science*, 100, pp.235–236.

growth of ASSAf, its evident productivity, and its high standing in the international community of academies, especially in Africa, eroded the contestation, except for a few hold-out groupings.

Last-gasp effort: Driving the machine against its will

Near the end of my long period of service as DVC at UCT, I began another enterprise that became my near full-time post-retirement project for a little over two years, from the middle of 2002. This was to gather together a number of nascent, but process-blocked, ideas for the consolidation of research in infectious disease and molecular medicine in the Faculties of Health Sciences and Science, in a single large-scale project to establish a university research institute (the Institute of Infectious Disease and Molecular Medicine, the IIDMM, now the IDM) that would dwarf previously realised examples of this sort, with between 20 and 30 principal investigators cooperatively sharing a single organisational and intellectually open space. The idea flew in the face of a formidable array of vested interests and long-entrenched rule-books, and took an enormous amount of advocacy, planning dexterity, resilience and collegiality (on the part of one's few institutional allies and the able researchers who became institute members), plus a big fundraising challenge to bring it to fruition.

I have included the IIDMM project in this reflection because it was initiated during my term as DVC, and because it reflects the enormous inertia in the decision-making machinery of a university that would have surely made it impossible to establish the institute, except under the personal project-direction of a recently retired senior official armed with the fullest inside knowledge of that machinery. I believed in the vision, shared it with the many fine scholars who saw its potential for opening up new opportunities and ways of working together, and simply pushed against all opposition until the IIDMM reached the launching stage when others took over direction and turned it into the largest and best-funded research enterprise at Africa's top-ranked University.

Concluding reflections

In writing this account of my experience as a university executive, I have tried to include just enough detail to permit readers to assess how this experience matches up with my introductory reflections on the requirements of this unusual kind of leadership. Each person who enters this demanding terrain will encounter a situation that has both unique and generic ingredients. The approach has to be adapted to meet the challenges as they are. If my account has made it seem that the circumstances in my own case were mostly of a special character, then I will be disappointed. What makes a contribution memorable (and fun) is the skilful turning of generic situations into unique ones, by seeing the job as essentially creative in nature and not bureaucratic or merely responsive to day-to-day diary demands.

Please don't sue me

Finally, I must say that I know full well that my career as a university leader was almost continuously controversial, and that there are some, perhaps many, who would contest my version of the key episodes, or, at least, see them in a very different light. I apologise to those (I hope they are few) who might be offended by my account. Memory is never completely reliable, and self-justification is common and self-delusion even more so. Perhaps I would approach the (unfortunately impossible) opportunity of a rerun differently, but not by much. It was far too exciting, and too intensely enjoyable, to do that.

chapter 3

Lessons for leadership in higher education

Brenda M. Gourley

Professor Brenda Gourley was the Vice-Chancellor (VC) of the University of Natal in South Africa for eight years. When she was appointed in 1994, she was South Africa's first female VC. In 2002, she was appointed the fourth VC of the Open University in the United Kingdom [UK], and she occupied that post for nearly eight years until 2009.

Gourley is a non-executive director of several boards and trusts, both in the public and private sectors, in the UK, Europe, the United States of America [USA] and South Africa. She currently chairs the Council for Education in the Commonwealth as well as the Board of Governors for the University of the World in the USA. She is a frequent speaker across the world – especially promoting the role of higher education in furthering social justice, civic engagement and the changing nature of higher education in the digital world – and is widely published.

She has been recognised for her achievements through awards, medals and prizes as well as 14 honorary degrees and fellowships from institutions on four continents. Gourley is a chartered accountant and Emeritus Professor of Finance and Accountancy.

There can be few jobs as stimulating and exhilarating as that of the Vice-Chancellor (VC) of a good, and reasonably large, university. You will seldom, if ever, be bored. You will meet fascinating people, work alongside extremely talented and creative people, and learn about their work. There is always good news to be found somewhere in the university: a discovery, a new book or article published, a new research programme funded, a new exhibition, a play – the list is endless – and part of your job is knowing about these things and celebrating the creativity they demonstrate.

You will be stretched in ways you could never have imagined and remain on a learning curve until the very last day of office. There are few things that will entirely prepare you for the intensity and relentlessness of the job. People see that part of the role that is relatively public, not the long evenings entertaining foreign and local guests, attending functions, writing speeches and articles, reading endless committee papers, catching up on correspondence, reading and all the things that never seem to find a place in the day's diary, to say nothing of travel and all the endurance that requires. Your spouse will see one part of your job, your personal assistant will have the best grasp of the commitments, and executive colleagues will see you in private and public meetings during the day and some evenings. Only you will know the whole picture – and only you can make the calls with respect to priorities and endless demands. Only you can really monitor your health and energy levels and call time when necessary. Only you can impose on yourself the discipline of reflection and learning, of seeking out opportunities, of listening, and much more besides.

As ever, it is possible to learn from others that have gone before you, to take advice and even counselling on your own aptitudes and skills, strengths and weaknesses. Such reflection should lead you to conclude that you need help in some areas and to seek it out. There is a genre of books written by retired presidents and VCs, and they are helpful. I hope that my reflections, grounded as they are in serving as VC in two universities, in two different countries, will also be helpful.

What did I learn?

Learning will take place at several levels and this chapter is organised to reflect different 'levels of learning', but, of course, some things impinge on every aspect of the role of the VC. The first level has to do with the personal attributes of the occupant of the post.

Attributes

There are, I believe, certain aspects of character and casts of mind that will determine whether you sink or swim. I have written about this elsewhere but will summarise here for ease of reference.[1] This is not about the mental 'furniture' of leadership like intellect, vision, knowledge, charisma and such attributes that some people have to a greater or lesser degree. People who seek to be leaders (or already are leaders) would do well to exercise and hone the attributes that they have and ponder what the absence of others might mean for their leadership.

My list is a personal one and some attributes are non-negotiable:

I.   *Integrity* is a non-negotiable. I believe that, to inspire confidence, there must be trust, and that, without integrity, there can be no trust. Such integrity should extend to every aspect of one's life and even to the reason for taking on the role in the first place: having integrity of purpose. Acting with integrity will give one an 'authenticity' which will define you and how you discharge your office. It will make life a lot easier for the people around you as well.

II.   *Courage.* It takes courage to stand out there on your own, to take positions that are sometimes unpopular, controversial and difficult; it takes courage to endure.

III. *Optimism.* People need their leaders to be optimistic, and cheerful. I used to make a habit of walking around the campuses as much as I could, stopping to have a chat with various people and generally trying to keep my eye on what was happening. I remember once, when the University was front-page news about some 'student riot' (that in fact only involved about 50 students of our then student body of 30 000), someone saying to me that they had read the newspaper and were horrified – and then they saw me walking across the campus, stopping to share a joke with someone and looking perfectly cheerful and he thought, 'things must be all right' and went back to his faculty to reassure them.

IV.   *Resilience.* One dictionary definition of resilience is 'the capacity to recover quickly from difficulties; toughness'.[2] One has to be able to take setbacks and one has to be able to handle stress. I am told I handle stress well. I do this by being clear in my mind what the

---

1   Kanwar, A., Ferreira, F. & Latchem, C. (eds) (2013) *Women and Leadership in Open and Distance Learning and Development* (Commonwealth of Learning: Vancouver).
2   http://www.oxforddictionaries.com/definition/english/resilience. Accessed 7 August 2015.

really important things in my life are. These all relate to people, specifically my family and friends. Student protests, for example, I did not find stressful. Annoying, difficult, demanding, but not stressful.

V.   *Self-reflectiveness.* The word speaks for itself, but it is not a quality one takes for granted. When one leads and manages a lot of people, inevitably there will be mistakes – theirs and your own. I used to ask myself and my colleagues what had been learnt from the mistake and what could be changed to ensure it did not happen again. There is a famous account of a Vice-President of a company making a mistake that cost the company a million dollars. He felt obliged to tender his resignation to the President. The President asked what he had learnt. On hearing the answer, he refused to accept the resignation on the grounds that the company had just spent a million dollars on staff development and wanted to see a return on the investment!

VI. *Capacity to listen.* It is impossible to underestimate the importance of listening. If one is not good at this, one had better practise. An African man told me once that his mother used to tell them as children that God gave them two ears, two eyes and one mouth – and that He intended them to be used in the right proportion. I have handed on that advice many times, and try to stick to it myself.

VII. *Decisiveness.* At the level of VC there are few decisions which are clear-cut. Anyone needs some time to cogitate over difficult decisions, but there comes a time when decisions have to be made. One cannot make the world less complicated than it is, but one can bring some resolution.

VIII. *Discipline.* This applies to many areas of one's life, but, in particular, to one's public behaviour. I have seen VCs lose their tempers in meetings and other public places. It is not acceptable. It demeans the person and the office. Anyone who cannot control his or her tongue should not be in office. I have to admit to losing my temper a couple of times (once in meeting with unions and another with students), and the strange thing is that, when I apologised to my deputies, they told me my reaction to the unreasonable behaviour that triggered the incident was overdue. It was of course viewed in the context that this was not a recurring behaviour. I still would rather I hadn't lost my temper. Discipline also extends to timekeeping. It is disrespectful and discourteous to people to keep people waiting.

IX. *Compassion.* A great deal of this job will be dealing with people. Inevitably there will be difficulties. I think the job needs to be done with one's head and one's heart. Of course there are legalities and rules which will constrain you, but err on the side of generosity and see the person, not just the situations. Kindness is remembered long after the incident that warranted such kindness.

X. *Capacity to compromise.* When one is a VC (I found this especially the case in my early years in South Africa from 1994), one spends an inordinate amount of time trying to resolve conflict of one sort or another – conflict with and between people, conflict with student organisations, and conflict with unions. I have found that there is seldom no good reason at all for a dispute. There will always be at least a kernel of truth in the cause of any dispute. No matter how much political posturing there may be, unions do not, in my experience, see it as being in their interests to take up issues that are entirely baseless. Spend time trying to find that nugget and spend time trying to find something to give way on. If each side can walk away with honour, you have a good outcome. 'Saving face' is seen as more important in some cultures than in others. In my experience, all people need to be treated in such a way that they retain their dignity. Contrast this with the need to win that a lot of people have. It is not helpful, and, indeed, often destructive to relationships.

XI. *A sense of humour.* Having a sense of humour will see one through life more easily, but in the role of VC it might well mean one survives intact as a person. It also means one will be able to diffuse tense situations and get things into perspective. Taking yourself too seriously is never a good idea anyway. Cultivate a sense of the ridiculous. It will get you through the day.

XII. *Composure.* One's ability to keep composed will be mightily tested. In South Africa during my time there as VC, there were rioting students, union protests, and boycotts of one sort or another. It would never do for the VC to be seen to be discomposed by these situations. When one is in a highly visible office, one needs to be aware that people read too much into the expressions that one displays – so you had better learn to control them. Staff members look to one to keep one's head 'when all about you are losing theirs'.[3]

Leading and managing talented people

The second level of learning is about the nature of leadership itself, and, in particular, about leading and managing creative people. One will not have many of the levers available to managers in the private sector, and such levers might well be inimical to a university environment. Even business environments know the value of participatory leadership, and this is what one can and should encourage across the institution. It is a generic type of leadership well suited to a university environment. It is when people do not show leadership, for whatever reason, at different levels in the organisation that one is in trouble.

Much has been written about leadership, and we know there are different kinds of leaders and that they can be equally effective. It is worth reading some of the literature in this domain. It will help you consider what kind of leader you aspire to be. I was much influenced by Peter Senge's book, *The Fifth Discipline*, which has been called one of the most influential books of the 20th century.[4] Not only did it strengthen my belief in systems thinking, but it also moulded my ideas about what kind of leadership was appropriate to the institution in which I found myself.

In this respect, I can only go on my own experience of several decades. First of all, I have always seen myself as a 'servant leader' – in the service of the creative people who can make a university truly great. If one can see oneself in this way, one will avoid some of the worst excesses we see in public life. I also saw my role as one of inspiring in staff a sense of mission and harnessing their talent in transforming the organisation, aligning resources to achieve that mission as well as their own goals, and keeping from them as much of the hassle and drudgery of regulatory regimes and bureaucracy as I possibly could. I was part of their support system, even their patron. I respected their particular talents and I cared for them as people. I was tolerant of mistakes and tried to encourage a culture of risk management rather than risk aversion. I tried hard to help them find connections and make partnerships and collaborations across the organisation, across the city, across other businesses, and across other universities. And I held

---

3   "If you can keep your head when all about you are losing theirs and blaming it on you", from the poem *If* by Rudyard Kipling.
4   Senge, P. (1990) *The Fifth Discipline – the Art & Practice of the Learning Organization* (Doubleday Business: New York).

fast to particular values and to the particular mission of the University. One always falls short of being the best in all the things one wants to be, but this is what I aimed for.

The leaders of universities are not quite the same as the leaders of other kinds of creative organisations. The hierarchies are different; the social contract, for want of a better phrase, is not the same. In many countries the academic has tenure and any leader who wishes to break that contract of tenure will have difficulty in doing so. How does one lead people who don't want to be managed? And with whom one has very few points of leverage? How does one attract and keep the right people who are becoming ever more important in an age when so much information is available and it is what one does with that information that counts? Everybody is chasing what Richard Florida has dubbed 'the creative class'.[5] In particular, universities are chasing the brightest and the best and their business is now global. Wildavsky writes that this scholarly marketplace is creating a new kind of world for higher education.[6] The questions raised pose issues that will define one's university. One will have to ponder and arrive at some practical strategies as well as casts of mind: a philosophy.

It seems to me that those who understand how to manage creativity in their people, who organise for creative results, and who willingly implement good new ideas will be successful. What can a VC do in this challenging environment? Does it matter to an institution what the leader does? After all, we now know that leadership is a shared activity and needs to be encouraged at all levels of the organisation. Having said that, I have seen institutions lose some of their best talent because of failures in the leadership to grasp the essence, not only of how talented people work, but also what motivates them. And the flight of talent destroys an organisation quicker than anyone can imagine. There are many business and university examples.

In order to do the subject of this reflections book justice, I think that it is important to understand something about truly talented, creative people:

I.   They are driven. It is no coincidence that Daniel Pink called his book, *Drive*.[7] John Lennon, in a 1964 ITV (Independent Television) interview made the comment: "We'll carry on writing music

---

5   Florida, R. (2011) *The Rise of the Creative Class Revisited* (Basic Books: New York).
6   Wildavsky, B. (2010) *The Great Brain Race – How Global Universities Are Reshaping the World* (Princeton University Press: Princeton).
7   Pink, D. H. (2001) *Drive – the Surprising Truth about What Motivates Us* (Canongate Books: Edinburgh).

forever, whatever else we're doing, because you can't just stop. You find yourself doing it whether you want to or not." Those of us who have worked with truly talented people recognise this characteristic instantly. The really good academics hardly have to be 'managed' at all. They drive themselves harder than you would ever drive them.

II.   They crave novelty. This is a compulsive condition to a creative spirit. They want to be in "places that feed their curiosity, delight their senses and reciprocate their compulsions".[8] Diversity is important to the novelty they seek. Torr tells us that, "in every single case and in every single city that has demonstrated any degree of cultural or scientific achievement, the presence of a sizeable population of economic migrants is a necessary condition for success".[9] It seems clear that the intersection of skills and perspectives (different world views) is a precondition for novelty. So, too, as Richard Florida points out, is tolerance and self-expression. The repression that existed in apartheid South Africa certainly had a negative effect on creativity.

III.   They seldom achieve their best in isolation or in small collectives. That is not to say that creativity cannot "be peaceful work performed in quiet solitude", but a significant number of creative people need to be with other talented people where ideas and dreams and visions and different world views can be shared and spark new paths, new things to research, new inventions.[10] People advise that we should try to create a galaxy rather than simply get hold of a star. Hire a star professor and aspiring doctoral candidates in that subject will flock to work with that person, but that star also wants to be with other catalysts to creativity, wants to be connected with other stars, other thought leaders, because they understand that a group of stars forms a galaxy and galaxies shine brightly enough to light the way for others to follow.[11] It's not a good idea to recruit one star. He/she will not stay the course, but will become frustrated and bored by having no one to test ideas, take ideas further, and provide different points of view. Given the

---

8   Torr, G. (2008) *Managing Creative People – Lessons in Leadership for the Ideas Economy* (John Wiley & Sons Ltd: Chichester), p.198.
9   Ibid., p. 202.
10 Larsson, U. (ed) (2002) *Cultures of Creativity. Birth of a 21st Century Museum* (Science History Publications: Massachusetts), p.11.
11 Ibid., p.61.

wonders of today's world, galaxies can be created by collaboratively working across the world and certainly by collaboratively working with other stars in business and other creative industries. Collaborative working also acts as a marketing 'pull' towards your organisation, because many more stars will get to know you and your institution this way. It follows that very small departments are not a good idea.

IV. They do not like being 'managed'. In general, academics conform to this stereotype in spades. They don't like being told what to do. They need to be persuaded and given time and opportunity to ask questions and interrogate any institutional strategy or change project – and they need to be heard – and they will find their own way. I cannot emphasise strongly enough how important it is to engage them in the grand project necessary to drive the trans-formation that is needed in higher education, a transformation that I think is vital to its survival.

V. They loathe bureaucracies and all the tedium of regulations and processes and procedures that are drowning universities in the Western world. Their inherent subversiveness abhors the business of management and we find it often drives them to the edges, even the margins, of the institution, and increasingly right out. They want "to pursue uncharted paths in their quest to achieve new levels of performance", and often institutional environments have so many policies and procedures that they constrain rather than facilitate.[12] Getting them to move from the margins to the centre of the institution is vital in this new world.

VI. They need creative space, resources and support, often emotional support, when projects and dreams take longer to bring to fruition than is expected, and sometimes they need help to effect closure. Support is often required in unexpected ways. My experience is that academics can be very unkind to one another and don't always give one another the support they need.

VII. Their loyalties are divided. Most academic staff members have divided loyalties. They are likely to have a greater loyalty to their discipline than to the institution where they work. The opinions

---

12 Hagel, J., Seely Brown, J. & Davison, L. (2010) *The Power of Pull: How Small Moves, Smartly Made, Can Set Big Things in Motion* (Basic Books: Philadelphia), p.185.

of their peers in their discipline are more important to them than the opinions of those that manage the university. This makes it really important to make your institution the one where they believe they will be supported to achieve their creative best.

VIII. They want flexibility and mobility. Truly talented people have lots of choices. Within reasonable limits, don't force them to give up all their opportunities. It might well work in your favour to have them working for you only some of their time: they will bring ideas from other places, and other groups in other places, inside or outside of the university sector. Keeping mobile is important to them, as it should be to you. Nowadays, collaborative research groups coalesce around a particular problem and break up when that problem is resolved. Your people need to be in those groups.

IX. They won't all look the same as your present cohort of staff. There is a saying that you cannot fix a problem using the tools that created it. There is an echo of that in staffing. When we look at the university sector in Europe, for example, we see it is male-dominated, quite elderly and white. It will, and does, replicate itself if left to its own devices. We know diversity is important and we need to be energetic and innovative in promoting it in our institutions if we are to attract the brightest and best wherever they may be. This is particularly important in South Africa, which is still experiencing the results of generations of inadequate education for some groups.

X. Lastly, and importantly, we need to understand that creative people are not all the same. They are likely to be a very diverse group of people.

If we have some idea of the attributes of clever, creative people, they give us strong pointers as to how leaders should manage and lead. For a start, I used to try to chair every professorial selection committee and chair all the promotion committees for senior posts as well. One has to have the right leadership in place throughout the university and the senior posts are vital. If we have some understanding of what motivates them, that, too, gives strong pointers as to how the institution should structure its processes and rewards.

Senior posts include those involved in the management of the business of the university: finance, human resources, estate management, technology management, the library, student affairs, and public affairs, to name the main portfolios. Getting the best people into these top jobs will be very important to ensure that your team has the credibility it needs to do the job. Recruit from the private sector as well as the public sector, and use head-hunters if you don't get the quality you need. Here, too, you are looking for talented people who have choices, and the university environment can be very varied and interesting – and therefore attractive.

What can leaders do?

The third level of learning is about some general features that pertain across the institution. Some are pertinent to the person, some to the university as a whole.

Those lessons pertinent to the person are as follows:

Communication

It is impossible to overemphasise the importance of communication. I have found that, no matter how much one thinks one is communicating, it is still not enough! Reaching people where they are, in a way that they understand, is the essence of good leadership. People who are able to construct narratives around the strategic priorities of the institution are at a huge advantage and the VC must work hard to construct such narratives. There is a book in the management literature called *The Power of Storytelling* by Holtje whose title speaks for itself.[13] There are many tools at one's disposal in this digital age. I always had a 'Vice-Chancellor's Newsletter' where I limited myself to the highlights of what staff needed to know as well as transmitting good news about individuals in the university who had brought credit to themselves and the institution. I also used it as a way to explain difficult issues facing the university. Some VCs blog or tweet. Beware of messages dashed off in a hurry. I always had my top team and communication staff members vet my messages to staff before I sent them out. I had a VC's website where people could pose questions, and get answers. We also posted on the website an abbreviated form of my diary. I had bimonthly forums on particular topics and all were invited: many attended via their computer screens and we took questions electronically. Screen-saver messages are useful for reaching a lot of people, but remember there are lots of staff members not sitting at computers. Find your own voice and use it often.

---

13 Holtje, J. (2011) *The Power of Storytelling. Captivate, Convince, or Convert any Business Audience Using Stories from Top CEOs* (Prentice Hall Press: New York).

Some leaders are not given to voicing praise. That is a mistake in my opinion. People need encouragement and one should seek to provide that encouragement wherever one can. Sometimes just writing a short note to express appreciation will do. At the University of Natal I learnt, many years later, that these came to be called 'Brenda's bouquets' and was surprised to hear that people kept them for years, sometimes on their desks. Give credit where credit is due and do that publicly as often as you can. Be generous. It is deeply appreciated.

Visibility

There is an expression in the literature of leadership called 'management by walking around'. One will never get familiar with an organisation if one doesn't get around. Visit people in their offices rather than always meeting in yours. Build time into your diary for visiting all parts of the university, academic as well as operational. Ask them to tell you about the issues they face and the successes they want you to know about. Listen carefully to what they say. See your job as removing obstacles from their paths so that they can be the best. Act on what they tell you and report back what you have done. Thank them for their help. Talk to gardeners and cleaners – you would be surprised at what they know. And never forget who really runs the show: the personal assistants and secretaries. I always spoke at their annual event and thoroughly enjoyed listening to their tales. Attend as many faculty and departmental functions and celebrations as you can manage. You will probably only be able to stay for a short time, say a few words, circulate a bit – it is surprising how much 'business' you can get done at functions and in the corridors, mainly sounding people out – and leave. Staff will appreciate you making the effort, and it gives you another chance to understand what is happening on the ground. If you are trusted, people will tell you things 'off the record', which is fine some of the time because one can get the internal auditor to follow up things brought to your attention without breaking confidences. All too often you will have to deal with issues brought to your attention informally by people who should be, but aren't, prepared to stand up publicly and give evidence. I don't find that acceptable.

Confidentiality

In my experience, confidentiality is seldom respected. No matter how often you remind people that the proceedings of this or that meeting are confidential, no matter how boldly you label the papers, no matter what you do, it seems people are unable to resist telling somebody, somewhere, whatever it is that is confidential. And people will employ any number of tactics to get you to divulge confidential matters. A sentence like, "I am so pleased to hear that so-and-so has been appointed" – it is true, she has – is one ploy to detect in your response affirmation of suspected outcomes or information passed on under the blanket of confidentiality. One has to be very guarded indeed. Don't for a moment assume that your emails will not end up as 'evidence', or that they will only be read by the addressee. Never write an email or letter in anger. Write it by all means, but don't push that 'send' button until the next day when you have had a chance to read it again. Confidentiality is not the only reason for following this piece of advice.

Privacy

When one is the VC of a university, one is inevitably a public figure. The university may well be one of the biggest employers in the district. This will be less so in a big place like London or some other capital cities, but it will certainly be so in smaller places. Whatever the case, one will find one's privacy invaded. If the VC's residence is on campus, it will be invaded even more. Don't imagine that there is no one on the beach who recognises one. The minute you step out of the door you are 'the Vice-Chancellor' and you are representing the institution and its values. People will come up to you at restaurants and the theatre and concerts and want to tell you all sorts of things that you would rather not hear at that time. Too bad for you. You will have to be polite and gracious and pleasant. That is part of your job.

Personal health

I really don't think this is a job that can be done by anybody unless they are in excellent health with a great deal of physical stamina. In my experience, the hours are extremely long (I very seldom worked less than 12 hours a day and very often more) and I slowed down to about five or six hours a day at the weekend: that was if I had no functions to attend. Some organisations require their executives to have regular medical checks. I think that is quite sensible but unlikely to be welcomed in a university culture. It will be up to you to get your health monitored. I used to find that if I took leave I would immediately get sick! Remove the adrenalin and that is what happens. It is not uncommon. It is also not uncommon for VCs to put on weight. There is an old joke about the difference between a VC and a supermarket trolley: you can fit more food into a VC. The fact is that there are so many lunches and dinners and receptions that one has to be disciplined to stay trim. You should book time into the diary to get some exercise. I had a personal trainer who had the flexibility to fit into my schedule rather than the other way around. That was invaluable. Pay attention. It affects the quality of your output.

Maintaining intellectual capital and support

One may be surprised to learn how much 'studying' has to be done. Not only is the world becoming more complex, but the world of higher education is also changing beyond all recognition. This is partly spurred by the technological revolution we have witnessed over the past two decades, but also by changing demographics and large forces like globalisation. Derek Bok, a long-serving President of Harvard University, wrote:

> Like so many others who have ventured down this path, I had no opportunity to study higher education in detail before finding myself consumed by its demands. Only after my active service ended did I find the time to read deeply about the subject that had already filled my life for a quarter of a century. Having done so, I often look back with some chagrin, realising how differently I might have acted had I understood then what I only came to appreciate much later.[14]

The fact is, if one wishes to do the job properly, one will have to read a lot, one will have to consult a lot, one will have to go to higher education and other conferences, and one will have to visit other universities in other educational systems. I subscribe to several international journals – educational publications (like *The Chronicle of Higher Education*), educational technology publications (like *Educause*), business management publications (like the *Harvard Business Review*) and general-interest ones (like *The Economist*). I read books and articles in the general domain of strategy, trends, leadership, and, of course, higher education. I belong to several online groups and follow the writings of particular people whose views I admire. I watch some people on TED talks as well.[15] I am emphasising this point because, no matter what, one is the strategist-in-chief of the university. If one misses the main trends, there can be no one else to blame but you.

You have undertaken a difficult job. You cannot know everything and you cannot always rely on people to advise you. You should at least consider getting yourself a mentor, not necessarily to meet regularly but at least from time to time when things are especially tough. There

---

14 Bok, D. (2013) *Higher Education in America* (Princeton University Press: Princeton), p.4.
15 TED is a non-profit devoted to ideas worth sharing: https://www.ted.com/. Accessed 7 August 2015.

are hardly any people inside the organisation with whom you can share some of the issues you face. Having a serious and experienced person to talk things through with you can be invaluable. Coaching could be important to your team as well, both as a team and individually. One would hope that at least one or two of them would aspire to be VCs, and part of one's job in managing them is to help them in that. I have mentored several people and been surprised at how appreciative they have been of the help and advice given.

One will inevitably have to deliver a lot of speeches. I found it essential to have some support in my office to assist me with this duty. I mainly needed background research done. Some of it was quite straightforward, some of it very demanding indeed. The person one will get to help with this will be very important. One will have to spend some time with her/him at the beginning so that the person can learn your 'voice', and, of course, one can never delegate the main message you aim to deliver for someone else to conceptualise, but get someone you must. I tried at one time to do without and I nearly fell over. I tried a professional speechwriter, but that didn't work for me at all. You would also do well to have some private coaching in technique and presentation. You may well be able to deliver a well-researched and thoughtful speech, but that is not enough. Unless one is very gifted, there will be room for improvement, and such improvement will pay handsome dividends. You need to be careful about the invitations you accept to present at conferences and in other academic forums. Some you accept because they will build the 'brand' of the university. Others you accept because you know they will stretch you – and, in the stretching, you will learn. There is nothing like having to articulate something to make you learn. Don't eschew these opportunities. Ask your colleagues to comment on your drafts, and share your learning where you can. Try to get material published. It makes it easier to hold others to publishing targets.

Financial literacy is something one simply has to have. If one is not strong in this domain, then I suggest you take a course at a business school or wherever. It is not something one can delegate. You also have to have faith in your chief financial officer. If you do not, you had better set about correcting the situation. The same goes for the registrar.

One had better be reasonably good at chairing meetings or you are going to waste an awful amount of your time and that of many others. This is a skill one can learn; see, for example, Robert's *Rules of Order*.[16]

---

16 Roberts, H. M. (2011) Roberts' *Rules of Order* (Da Capo Press: Boston).

It hardly needs emphasising, but the secretarial and office support one needs has to be of the highest calibre. I was exceptionally fortunate in this respect and remain to this day deeply appreciative of the people in my office whose efficiency and perceptiveness made all the difference. One cannot afford to settle for less.

Those lessons pertinent to the university as a whole are as follows:

About teams

There is a lot written in the management literature about the importance of teams and the team-building that goes into making a good team. That is no surprise, because no one person can attend to all the tasks that need attention. Any VC will only be as good as the team around him/her. Anyone who thinks otherwise is delusional. I was lucky in having some extraordinarily good people on my teams.

It follows that the effectiveness of the team one has at the executive level will be crucial to the success of the organisation. Ineffectiveness, or worse, dysfunctionality will inflict a high cost on the institution. It behoves one to concentrate, on a continuing basis, on ensuring that effectiveness. One should arrive at a code of conduct together with your team, and hold one another to its principles. One should be very clear as to what one expects – both in objective-setting and behaviour. I never asked of anyone more than I was ready to give of myself. I was always completely honest with my colleagues. In my opinion this is essential to building not just trust but confidence – one cannot have one without the other. My colleagues could count on me having high expectations of them, carefully framed in collaboration with them, but they could also count on my loyalty and support, even if everything did not go according to plan. I also expected them to be loyal to one another. The jobs they have to do are difficult enough without having to watch one's back all the time. If there were occasions when less than good conduct was apparent, I spoke to people privately, not in front of others. I have seen so many people in positions of authority publicly humiliate staff members. This is not the way to build loyalty, support or any other positive relationship. Time spent on team-building and team maintenance will never be wasted.

I have read a lot of literature on team-building and learnt a lot in the process. I think team-building exercises are necessary from time to time, and I usually used outside facilitators to run such events. Such facilitators should be selected with care. In the hurly-burly of university life, the members of the executive have very little time together that is not dominated by an agenda or need to reach a decision. Regular executive meetings are essential, as is building in some time to get to know one another. The skill of the facilitation will often dictate whether those participating in team-building exercises find the time well spent or not. I would avoid expensive and prolonged events.

Fostering a democratic culture

Musil reminds us that "higher education is a key site of possibility and promise", a place where we can turn democratic aspirations into democratic practice.[17] I believe it behoves universities to behave in such a way as to make a contribution to a working democracy, more especially in a new democracy like South Africa. I have also found that universities are not as democratic as they would have you believe. One only needs to look at their record with respect to the promotion of women. It is only in the last few decades that they even admitted women into their august leadership circles. It would seem that being sites of learning characterised by critical thinking, logic and moral philosophising somehow managed to avoid reflection on the rights and wrongs of discrimination against women. Universities are the nurseries for tomorrow's leaders, which adds another dimension to being seen to act out the principles of the causes we espouse.

Acting out democratic principles starts with the VC. It is a constant source of amazement to me how autocratic many VCs are. This is inappropriate, even in terms of good management practice, not least in a university setting where our aspirations should be loftier.

In the acting out of democratic principles, VCs need to interrogate not only their governance and management, but also their educational practice: their curriculum, research and community engagement. It is difficult to propound the notion that a university fosters a democratic culture when its curriculum deals only with esoteric matters far removed from the reality in which its students live and work. Similarly, a research agenda that ignores the issues and concerns of the society in which the university is embedded is hardly nurturing of the characteristics of a robust democracy: especially active engagement. Furthermore, engagement with the society in which the university is sustained is an important and potent signal to the students and staff that good citizenship requires active participation. We gave enormous attention to community, business and non-governmental organisation (NGO) relationships and the University benefitted from this. It changed the nature of conversations about curriculum and about research. Their critiques even helped develop the quality of our strategy-planning

---

17 Beckham, E. F. (2000) *Diversity, Democracy and Higher Education: A View from Three Nations* (Association of American Colleges and Universities: Washington DC).

exercises. Given the benefits of technology, we now have large virtual communities as well, and there are many demonstrations of what the power of information and group action can achieve, stimulated by the interconnected power of our web users.

Finally, the university's public face must be one that is visible and active in the spaces provided by democratic societies. Staff and students must experience on an ongoing basis the meaning of free speech, open debate and vigorous but respectful exchange of ideas and, importantly, disagreement. Universities must be places where students, staff and members of the public learn to participate in order to become the informed citizens they need to be if democracy is to flourish. University leaders need to demonstrate their commitment to these ideals by prompting debate, being visible when it is important and taking a stand where it is necessary to do so, always appealing to the best in the human spirit, and making it difficult for the worst to flourish. This is the enactment of true citizenship.

Process

There is nothing that will destroy the staff's trust in the university more surely than bad processes. It is wise to spend some time understanding what the main processes are, and the rules that are in place to support them. In the process of trying to understand them, one is likely to be surprised at how opaque some of them are. These one should aim to fix. One will often find oneself having to defend them so you had better believe they are fair and reasonable. If they are fair and reasonable, you must rely on them. One cannot be in all parts of the management structure at once. Just because a process has been in place for a long time doesn't make it fit for purpose in current conditions. In fact, it almost certainly is not. This is especially so in the technological world we live in. Lots of processes can be speeded up if done electronically. This will reduce the general frustration academics have with administrative processes, to say nothing of creating a more efficient organisation.

The other thing that will destroy staff's trust is you not abiding by the processes. One must be meticulous in following them. One cannot expect others to follow them if you do not. One cannot claim ignorance. One's integrity will be on the line.

Governance and governors

It is vital that the university has in place carefully constructed governing structures with clear mandates. It is crucial also that the people who are elected or appointed to the various committees are the best they can be, are properly representative (diverse) and are well informed as to the role they are required to play and how to play it. Carefully constructed induction processes and codes of conduct can help in this regard.

One must play an active role in ensuring that good representation is achieved. Calls for nomination should explicitly outline the skills, knowledge and experience needed to fulfil the tasks of the relevant committee. Indeed, a nominations committee is often a useful instrument for examination of such matters and members undertake the task of seeking out people who would not necessarily make themselves available.

The role of the chair of any particular committee should not be underestimated. A bad chair may not only waste people's time, but may also allow the agenda to be hijacked. A strong and skilled chair will negotiate any divisions that might arise and hold the centre. Terms of reference have to be understood and it may well be useful to offer training in improving skills in this matter.

The role of the Chair of Council merits special mention. It is crucial that the person in this office is clear about what the council can and does expect from management and where the council should not get involved. No committee can 'manage'; only people can manage. No council can 'manage' the university; nor should it seek to do so. It can and must, however, set up processes by which it can judge whether the strategic priorities upon which it has agreed are being implemented.

The relationship between the Chair of Council and the VC is an important one, and it behoves both individuals to ensure they have a good understanding of each other's role and go to some lengths to cultivate and maintain a good working relationship.

Governance arrangements are not always satisfactory and, in my experience, need changing from time to time. They should be as streamlined as possible, with as little repetition in the terms of reference of subcommittees as possible. There should be as few of the latter as possible. They should also be reasonable in their size of membership. A review from time to time often seems to reveal ways in which processes can be improved and time can be saved.

Relationships and networks

I sometimes think the whole of life depends on the quality of one's relationships. They matter in your personal life and they matter in your professional life as well. They need to be nurtured and maintained and generally kept in good repair. If one is 'bad' at this for some reason, one will have a difficult time doing this job. I remember watching a VC persuade a senate to vote for something they really were not inclined to accept. They did so because the VC was such a good and decent person; they liked him and gave him the benefit of the doubt. When one's role is persuading and influencing rather than ordering, one needs some personal connection to people. Personal connections in large organisations require time and nurturing. I am lucky because I genuinely like people, and I find them, and what drives them, endlessly fascinating. I also have a good memory for names and faces. That helps. There are ways in which one can improve this skill, and if one hasn't got it, I would recommend trying them.

I think it is a mistake to underestimate the value of entertaining in the building of relationships. It takes place at several levels: inviting people to dinners, lunches and receptions is one way of getting people to feel part of the university community. This includes people within the university, council members, people in the town where the university is located, partners in research or other endeavours, and important people in the community who could be disposed to act as ambassadors for the university or even donors. Having an events organiser who makes sure that the occasions go well is crucial to making one's life easier.

Good relationships build trust. If anything goes wrong or there is a misunderstanding, one can then pick up the phone or go and see somebody to sort things out. I worked hard on relationships and, in the process, I met wonderful people, some of whom became personal friends, and many of whom displayed great loyalty to the University. It was one of the great pleasures of the job.

Fundraising

The VC is inevitably the fundraiser-in-chief. Some VCs are spectacularly good at this. The first hurdle to overcome is the reluctance to ask. I never felt that reluctance, but many do. One is not asking for oneself; one is asking for the university or the project. The second hurdle is to have an efficient team behind one in the fundraising operation. Asking people to support projects that do not match their stated mission is wasting their time and yours. One needs good data in the office which matches project with donor. The third hurdle is making sure one has good proposals. This last is often the key. I never asked for something that I didn't genuinely believe the university could not fund out of its own resources. Getting the university community to come up with proposals was difficult at the beginning, but, as people became used to competing, used to the idea that not every proposal would find funding and used to being more entrepreneurial, I used to set off on my trips with a briefcase full of them. They often got funded from surprising sources. I once set off to get funding for a Chair in Information Technology (IT) and came away with a funded Chair in Ethics. One has to have a good knowledge of what is in the briefcase.

Alumni are often an important element in the fundraising business. I got one of the biggest donations the University had received because research in the office turned up an alumnus who had done extremely well and had no heirs. My meeting with him was followed by a visit to his old faculty and what he saw impressed him so much he changed his will. Keeping good alumni records is an essential part of this business. Alumni are important in other ways – they are the university's natural ambassadors. In this day of easy electronic communication it is a simple matter keeping them informed and enthusiastic about their alma mater. There will be community leaders amongst them. Seek them out and bring them into the life of the university. They will surprise you.

Setting the agenda: Strategy and scenarios

This is the fourth level of learning. The days are gone when strategy was in the hands of a few people in the university. The fierce competitiveness that has now invaded higher education as well as the competition for the best staff and students has made a difference, but the declining resource per student head has probably made the biggest difference of all. It is not sensible to allocate scarce resources without agreeing on strategic priorities, unless one wants to abandon any notion of quality. Agreeing on strategic priorities means making choices, often tough choices. You haven't got a strategy until you know what you are not going to do. And you won't have a successful strategy unless you engage as many parts of the university as possible in its construction.

One device used to encourage this attention has gained currency in some quarters over the last decade. It is known as 'scenario-based strategic planning'. It turns out to be one of the best tools available for drawing out the social creativity of communities and engaging them in strategic conversations. It is those strategic conversations that are vital to the health of an organisation.

Strategic conversation will include pondering the very nature of the university and what it wishes for the student experience, what it wishes to achieve in the community in which it is sustained, and where it wishes to focus its research efforts. It is unwise to make this an inward-facing exercise. One needs as many external perspectives as possible, and finding a way to bring different people from different walks of life into the process will make it richer and more credible.

Research strategy, apart from reflecting a strong focus and being as multidisciplinary as possible, should not only build from strength but should also reflect what the university sees itself contributing to regional, national and even global issues. In KwaZulu-Natal, we were physically located in the epicentre of the HIV/Aids pandemic. It would have been unconscionable if the University were not particularly strong in its research endeavour in this matter – and it is. Research has also changed by virtue of so many digitised assets (libraries, art collections, museums, 'big data' banks, to mention just some) and these, combined with phenomenal computer power, mean we can ask questions we couldn't ask before. We can also assemble collaborative groups at almost zero cost. So research is not limited to that which can be done only with the staff one has on one's payroll but also with those in collaborations.

It bears repeating that technology and all it has enabled has changed the world of higher education completely. Universities used to describe themselves as places where knowledge was produced, stored and disseminated. You could almost describe the Internet in those terms. Without pursuing the argument, it suffices to make the point that the harnessing of technology to the research as well as the teaching and learning endeavour is fundamental in the 21st century. Innovation in its use needs to find its place in the strategic thinking of the university.

The setting of strategic priorities cannot take place only at the highest level in the university. Faculties and administrative divisions all need to reflect on their place in the overall direction set and work out their strategies for making sure they contribute to the whole.

Management and implementation

This is the fifth level of learning.

It is my experience that people find it much more interesting dreaming up strategic priorities than finding ways to implement them; so it is, in many ways. Implementation and keeping the show on the road is called 'management'. Academics often sneer at it and go on about 'managerialism' taking over higher education. The fact of the matter is that, if one doesn't 'manage' the institution in a sensible way, most of the strategic imperatives will get lost, and funding will be misused to no purpose. The university needs people who are what Myers–Briggs called 'implementers/finishers'. Stamina, determination, persistence and even sheer guts will play their part here. You will find the built-in inertia in the system extremely difficult, and the cynics will wait for you to give up and go away, like others before have done. There are several keys to ensuring successful implementation of strategy:

I.   Make sure the strategic priorities are properly funded. If resources are not allocated in a manner consistent with the priorities, any time spent on setting those priorities will have been wasted and the process discredited. You will not find support for your next round of planning.

II. Make as much management as possible evidence-based. I came from a private-sector background (I am a chartered accountant by profession) and I remain amazed by how some people in universities think they can manage by instinct rather than reason. Managers must not report that everything is going all right in their division without any evidence to back them up. One would think that there would be more respect for evidence in a university environment, but it is sometimes hard work dragging it out of some parts of the operation. While universities are not businesses in the ordinary sense of the word, there is still every reason for them to be businesslike and a businesslike approach should be apparent in all the operational activities of the institution – what some would call a 'value for money' approach. One part of this exercise is deciding what should be done by the institution itself and what could or should be outsourced. The past few years have demonstrated that there is very little that cannot be outsourced – think of Massive Open Online Courses (MOOCs), and, if something can be done better by some other entity at a lower price, there had better be a good reason for using university money otherwise.

It is vital to be alert to performance indicators and benchmarking, and the wealth of data that is now quite easy to collect. There is an old management maxim to the effect that if one want something managed, then it had better be measured, with the caution that one had better be careful about what one measures because what gets measured gets managed – and compared. I had a system of 'traffic lights' instituted (using the green, amber and red symbols) to catalogue leading indicators signalling 'trouble' ahead or at least matters which needed management attention before a budgeted or predicted outcome was likely to change. As a way of managing risk, if nothing else, it is effective in alerting one to areas that need attention. There is now a whole industry in learning analytics which is not only a rich seam of data for educators to further their understanding of how people learn, but is also vital to understanding how the attrition rates amongst students can be reduced. Attrition rates have been unacceptably high for too long. Benchmarking is also valuable in this context. And it is best used not as a tool with which to beat people. One wants them to know how good they are. The only way they will do that is by comparison.

III. Make sure the systems are as sophisticated as possible in their use of technology. One's research profile will depend on sophistication of one sort; one's administration on another; one's teaching and learning systems on yet another. The Open University has a sophisticated customer relations management system, developed and used mostly in the private sector, to improve student support and collect data. Even curriculum planning is understood, in these days of open and distance learning being offered by more and more of the traditional institutions, to need more careful, and more centralised, attention to the 'product' upon which so much else depends. All institutions are in a 'market' – regional, national and even global – and that market has to be monitored, competitors have to be monitored, and the nature and profile of its 'customers' have to be analysed and understood.

IV. Make sure one has the right people to carry out agreed measures of implementation. Academic faculties, for example, should be led by strong deans who have the necessary competencies, knowledge and experience to manage the faculty and deliver on priorities. Deans elected in some kind of popularity contest without any regard for the specifics of what the job entails can hardly be expected to cope adequately with what is often an extremely challenging position. They need to be adequately rewarded, managed and supported, with additional training in areas where they need it. Similarly, the support functions in the university need to be strongly led. Insisting on recruiting only from the sector is not helpful. Indeed, I think it is important to recruit from the private sector where appropriate. The marketing operation, the IT and a host of others are often headed up in The Open University by people who earned their stripes in the private sector and brought that experience to the University.

V. Make sure there is proper performance management in place. Performance management has a bad name in universities, where it is far too seldom practised, and elsewhere mostly because it is so poorly executed. It is not some punitive exercise designed to threaten and depress. It is much more about being clear about what is expected, arriving at goals in a consultative mode, and then giving feedback and encouragement. It is not even remotely possible to get the strategic priorities of the university enacted throughout the organisation unless some way is found of aligning individual goals with those of the organisation. It turns out that many people are not particularly good at this aspect of management. Make sure that they receive the help they need to improve.

There is a saying attributed to Jim Collins that, for an organisation to be successful, one needs to get the right people on the bus and the wrong people off the bus.[18] In my experience, people find the second part of this aphorism very difficult to effect. It is difficult to do. I haven't had to do it very often and in each case my regret was that I had not acted sooner. Nobody gains from the prolonged agony of someone who finds himself or herself in the wrong job. Do it as kindly as possible and make sure you follow the right protocols.

VI. Invest heavily in staff development. New strategic priorities often require reorientation and staff may well need help. Tougher management processes also make new demands. In particular, fast-changing technologies mean that there needs to be a heavy investment in development if staff members are to improve their skills and harness the technologies to the objectives of the university.

VII. Pay attention to risk. One should be required to keep a risk register as a normal expectation of good governance. It should not be seen as an imposition. It is a valuable prism through which to see the various aspects of what the university does. Use it as a means of growth and reflection. It seems to me that most university people are very risk-averse. This is not helpful in the world in which we now find ourselves. The focus must be on risk management, not risk aversion. It is an important difference.

The actions I am describing should result in at least some of the competencies that make an organisation *reflective, analytical and resilient* for the volatile times of today. In the process they also help with the business of culture change.

---

18 Collins, J. (2001) *Good to Great: Why Some Companies Make the Leap…and Others Don't* (Harper Collins: New York).

In conclusion

Higher education is going through what I would call 'seismic' change, probably the greatest change in its long history. Steering the organisation in the next decades will not be easy, but it will be a very important task, even a privilege.

Ronald Heifetz has this to say:

> Leadership oftentimes is a passionate and consuming activity. People need inspiration and drive to step out into a void, which only later is recognised as a place of creativity and development. So strong are the emotions of leadership, they can overwhelm the person who has not developed a sufficiently broad sense of purpose ... the capacity to find the values that make risk-taking meaningful.[19]

He goes on to make the point that preserving a sense of purpose helps one take setbacks and failures in one's stride. Sometimes, he reminds us, we have to give up on an organisational or political situation. We need the capacity and personal freedom to change or we risk disorientation and despair. Better we change than we give up leading.

---

19 Heifetz, R. (1994) *Leadership without Easy Answers* (Harvard University Press: Cambridge), p.274.

chapter 4

Values and people:
Backbone of the academic institution

Brian Figaji

Professor Brian Figaji was the Principal and Vice-Chancellor [VC] of the Peninsula Technikon in Cape Town from 1994 to December 2004. In January 2005, the Cape Technikon and Peninsula Technikon merged to form the Cape Peninsula University of Technology [CPUT]. Figaji obtained a Bachelor of Science Degree from the University of the Western Cape [UWC], a BSc Degree in Engineering from the University of Cape Town [UCT], a Diploma in Tertiary Education from the University of South Africa [UNISA], and a Graduate Diploma in Engineering and a Master of Education in Administration, Planning and Social Policy from Harvard University. He started his career in education and went into engineering, gravitating back to education almost by default. His intention initially was to become a teacher, which he did for one year, before working in industry for 12 years. He was thereafter appointed Acting Head of the College for Advanced Education which, later changed its name to Peninsula Technikon [Pentech], which he led until its merger.

He was an active Scout. At 18, he became a Junior Adult Leader, and, in 1975, an Assistant Divisional Commissioner. In 1977, he played a crucial role in amalgamating the four Scouting Movements into one united organisation for all, regardless of race or religion.

His professional activities are diverse. He was a Vice-President of the Engineering Council of South Africa; he is a Fellow of both the Academy of Engineers, and the South African Institute of Civil Engineers. In 2005, Professor Figaji was appointed to represent South Africa on the Executive Board of the United Nations Educational, Scientific and Cultural Organization [UNESCO] in Paris. He has also been appointed by the President to serve on the Advisory Board for National Orders.

He received an Honorary Doctorate of Humane Letters in 2001 from the California State University, Hayward, and an Honorary Degree of Doctor of Education from Coventry University in the United Kingdom [UK] in 2002.

This chapter is based on an interview conducted by Denyse Webbstock and Neo Lekgotla *laga* Ramoupi on 12 February 2014 in Cape Town.

W e opened the interview by asking Professor Figaji to reflect broadly on his academic leadership. His immediate response was to laugh, and say:

There are two things that I hold dear. One is you must love the students and regard them as your own children, because then you see the job in a completely different light. That is why I have a bit of a phobia about these institutions that have about 40 000 students, particularly in South Africa when you are going through a process of transition. With this first generation of higher education young people, you've got to be able to interact with them. That is why I was convinced that when we reached 12 000 students at Pentech [Peninsula Technikon] we should throw away the keys of the front gate. While a lot of our fellow institutions were opening up satellite campuses, we made a conscious decision that the only satellite campuses would be those that required us to locate the students nearer to facilities like radiography and dental technology in the hospital and other specialist facilities. Other than that, we would not establish satellite campuses. So our sister campus, Cape Technikon, had a number of satellite campuses; and we chose not to have them.

The second aspect that he felt was important in his academic leadership, related to the first, was the human side. He was always convinced that he needed to demonstrate that he could connect with the students and staff. Fortunately, his predecessor had developed a range of practices that he continued; for example, scheduled meetings between the Students' Representative Council (SRC) and management, which included the Vice-Chancellor (VC) and the deputies. These were strategic, not crisis, meetings about where they saw the institution going, why students were conducting themselves in a particular way, and so on. These scheduled meetings provided the opportunity for management to develop the student leadership and to set values: "We were pretty strong about values; we had the Vision, Mission and Institutional Values printed and framed and put up in all the offices and most of the public spaces." However, Figaji and his team were convinced that students would take little notice unless the leadership talked about, and demonstrated, their belief in the values. At graduation, when he welcomed new students, or when he talked to the SRC, he would always relate the conversation back to the values. As the VC of the institution, he used to say to the students that sexual harassment and any other form of violence would result in their expulsion, because it violated the whole notion of mutual respect, one of the core values of the institution. He told the first-year students every year: "I will pay for your flight back home if you are found guilty of violating the value of mutual respect." He continued:

> As the leader you have to demonstrate that you personally adhere to the values and that you respect the students, cleaners and gardeners. Your example will eventually convince others. And when the SRC members start to talk to other students about values, then you finally feel that you are winning. This is behavioural change and by its nature it is long-term stuff.

Figaji also thought that the VC of the institution should be visible on the campus to students.

> You should be seen in the courtyard speaking to your students ... so that students can identify with you and the institution. I really believe that if you have that interaction, there is a line which students will not cross. ... I don't know if there is a sense now that students have become more violent, but we did not have any serious event involving damage to property. Let me just step back from that; there were two incidents.

In the first incident:

> On a Monday morning, I got to campus and found graffiti on the wall between the administration building and the sports hall. It was not a lot, but it was visible, and clearly someone chose to vent some anger through this act, which was a violation of our space. I get to work early, at 7am, and I got there first and saw it. I wanted to make a big public fuss about this so that it could serve as a deterrent. I waited for 8:30am when I knew that all the students would be on campus and called the senior managers and some staff outside to the graffiti for a meeting in the courtyard. With the students walking by and some stopping to watch us, we discussed this violation of our property. I made it obvious so that many passers-by would have heard that we were waiting for the police to arrive. I had some people take photographs and I asked to see the SRC about this event. I chose to get a cleaning

company to come in at lunchtime to clean the graffiti so that there would be maximum awareness amongst the students. I also got our own security to ask students if they saw anyone suspicious who could have been involved. We made a huge fuss to demonstrate that we disapproved of this violation. So there was a degree of panic on campus. We did not find anyone, but it sent out a message that there would be consequences.

The second incident was at the Pentech administration building. Students came in marching. One of them accidently knocked a picture off the wall and the glass broke. I went to the SRC and they were very quick to admit that it was an accident, because they knew that there was a very low tolerance threshold for property damage.

I don't think we draw the line clearly enough between what is right and wrong or, put differently, between what is acceptable behaviour and what is not. Students are like our own children; they will test the boundaries and push the limits and we have to hold the line firmly, but with love.

On the question of mutual respect, Figaji related the tussle between the Pan Africanist Students' Movement of Azania (PASMA) and the South African Students' Congress (SASCO) for election to the SRC. PASMA members campaigned hard and won the election and SASCO members were furious. The SASCO members somehow got hold of the keys to the SRC offices and locked some PASMA members inside the SRC office. Without any keys visible, the SASCO members were standing in a circle in the cafeteria singing freedom songs. Staff from Student Affairs tried to obtain the keys to the offices to free the trapped students, but to no avail. Figaji was very unhappy about this action because it was, in effect, holding people hostage. He personally went into the circle of singing students in the cafeteria and demanded the keys. When no keys were produced, he gave them 20 minutes to produce them, failing which he would call the police and lay a charge against anyone found with the keys. After 15 minutes, the SRC office doors were unlocked and the students set free. The students knew that he was not just threatening them, but that he would call the police and lay a charge.

The institutional leadership was always sympathetic to the students, and would make every effort to attend student events. For example, when students invited the VC to the Sunday evening church service, he would always attend, even though he had to fight with them to start on time. Eventually, he developed a rule that, if they were more than 15 minutes late, he would leave. Figaji felt that it was important to value student events. They knew that they could turn to him for help and, if it were possible, he would help them as he would his own children. This bred a level of respect, which endured during the most difficult student protests.

Figaji's view was that student protests were often triggered by leadership struggles among them. During one such incident, the students carried mattresses to Figaji's office during a residence protest. Management had decided to replace the mattresses in the residences and were buying them in batches, residence by residence. Student leadership in the residences came under pressure as a result of a rumour that management was not going to buy mattresses for all the residences. Figaji called them to a meeting and explained the procedure for the purchasing of residences' mattresses, which he thought had not been properly communicated. He sat down with the students and made arrangements and compromises in the purchasing pattern. As this satisfied the student leadership, they called off the protest.

Figaji illustrates with a few more examples how he dealt with the challenges posed by his students, which tested his commitment to the institutional values of mutual respect, honesty and integrity:

> One afternoon I was in Johannesburg, and I got a call that there was some unhappiness on campus ... and the students wanted to meet me on that day. Students often tend to show their strength by making demands even if it is out of character for the individual, or unnecessary. It does not help if the VC has an ego; you have to be available and listen. I told the students that I am on the 5pm flight back to Cape Town and they said, "But we must see you today!" I told them I would see them on campus after I landed in Cape Town that afternoon. I got there, and there was a large contingent to meet me. The student leadership joined me in a room, while the others waited outside. It turned out to be a simple matter of a misunderstanding, which was easily resolved. I think the real test was to establish whether I regarded their matters as important enough that it warranted me coming to campus before going home. I did not know this at the time, but apparently I passed that test.

In another instance, he explains how he plucked up the courage to expel an SRC president:

> I was very concerned about this whole matter, since this leader had significant student support on campus. His mother was an MP [Member of Parliament] and the family was very well connected politically. I

had been to his mother's house because he had been in trouble before, and we had resolved that situation. A year later, he became SRC president. He was charismatic and had a strong following, but I think the students knew that he pushed the boundaries. He did something in the residences and we had a disciplinary hearing and he was found guilty. He was barred from going into the residence. Security complained that he went in and out of the residences with impunity, telling them that he was in charge there. We had another disciplinary hearing, found him guilty and sentenced him. He violated his sentence again. That was the second time. Then I was told he had stayed in the residences over the Easter holidays.

This was too serious a test. He had violated two disciplinary hearings. The Thursday we returned from holidays I called the deans to a meeting and I told them I wanted to expel the SRC president. They were all fed up with him, but expressed concern that this would cause instability on campus. It was important that we did this correctly, otherwise it could come back to haunt us. So we had to prepare a plan of action. The deans would ensure that students [were] invited to attend a meeting where I would make an announcement. I sent the institutional driver to fetch him from his home for a meeting with me. When he arrived in my office, I told him in the presence of a witness what the charges were. He agreed that he had stayed in the residence. I then handed him a letter saying, among other things, "I am expelling you from the institution". When he saw the letter he realised this was real. He started crying, saying, "What is my mother going to say about this?" I told him he should have thought about that before. I told him that if he came onto campus, I would have him arrested for trespassing. I then told Security to escort him off the campus.

Figaji told the student body that he had taken a big decision that might shock them; that he had expelled the SRC president. He spelt out the reasons. He said he understood that many of the students still supported him. He told them that he had considered that too, and would deal with any student action should it arise.

I then had a meeting with the matrons of all the residences and told them to be alert, and if there [was] any student gathering of any sort, they must call me at my home. That was a Friday; I have never had such a long weekend in my life. (Laughing). I spent a nervous weekend worrying about what could happen on Monday. Fortunately nothing happened.

Figaji's reflection so far had been on academic leadership that had been student-focused. We asked him about the staff. He replied:

I don't know if we were too liberal with the staff or gave them too much space. But I think sometimes when I look back at how staff behaved at other [higher education] institutions, they appeared to be acquiescent. Staff unions were rather inactive. Whereas, during my time at our institution, the union was very active; I was given quite a hard time. I think they did not like the fact that I saw things in … black and white terms on … staff matters. But even with the staff union we had formal quarterly meetings with minutes about matters institutional. I sometimes think that the union took advantage of our accommodating stance. My last year at the institution was quite fiery with the union because they accused me of dishonesty, and given that this was one of our core values, I was furious and formally charged all the executive members of the union. One union member wrote the article that contained this accusation, but the Exco [Executive Committee] members would not distance themselves from the content of the article and chose to stand by their colleague. This left me no option but to take disciplinary action against them all. After the disciplinary hearings had commenced, the union realised that they were in trouble and so they negotiated a settlement which included a public apology sent to all staff and printed in the local press.

One consolation was that, after I had left the institution, I met the union Chair at an inaugural lecture that we both attended. We knew each other quite well, despite our differences, and he said to me, "I must tell you, I know it is not a consolation but we did the wrong thing, we were unfair to you, and I am sorry about it". That gave me some peace of mind.

Figaji and his management team made good use of the available external programmes to provide staff with opportunities for further study. They sent staff members overseas for master's and doctoral studies. Pentech at the time had a reasonably young staff. One of the impediments was that staff did not always have enough accrued leave to use for study purposes. Management developed a system where they gave deserving staff their study leave in advance so they could pursue overseas study. This would tie the staff to the institution for some years until they had worked off their study leave after their return. In this way, Pentech maximised the study opportunities afforded by the American-funded Tertiary Education Linkages Project (TELP).

We were struck by these anecdotes about managing individual colleagues and asked Figaji whether this did not also have a downside:

> We were a relatively small campus so it was possible to know all the staff and all the student leaders, but also to know many students by just talking to them in the passages and courtyards. I told you about some of the events that I was directly involved with, but there are many others that were satisfactorily dealt with by the other senior managers. On the question of staff development, I was very hands-on because we were a very young staff and we needed to increase our staff qualifications very significantly. I know some staff found it irritating that I knew so much about what was happening on campus, but it was because I walked around and spoke to people at random and I believed it was my business to know. The only real downside is that you may unwittingly undermine a dean or a manager, but this is easily resolved if you as VC are prepared to apologise should this happen.
>
> The one thing that gives me a great deal of satisfaction is that some of my former students have internalised the value system. One of them wrote a newspaper article, and I wrote to him and said, "I am impressed with the stance you took because it is really value-based". And he wrote back to me and said, "How can I have missed it with all those lectures on values you gave us!"

Institutional mergers

Not everyone welcomed the institutional mergers that the Minister of Education introduced in higher education. Figaji expresses his view:

> The merger between Pentech and Cape Tech set to take effect from 1 January 2005 was the reason I left the university. I told my Council in March 2004 that I was going to leave at the end of 2004.

Figaji explained that he fundamentally disagreed with the mergers, which he saw as forced and politically motivated. He spoke out against the mergers, but in the end decided to leave the institution. Figaji explained further how:

> ...the merger precipitated other tensions on campus. Staff had requested that we offer them retrenchment packages before the merger took effect, but one of the principles of the merger was that no one would lose their job. Based on this principle, I refused to offer any staff a retrenchment package. However, it was clear that there could

be only one Vice-Chancellor for the merged institution and, given that I was opposed to the concept, I was adamant that I was going to leave. So when my Council offered me a severance package, the union objected and this gave rise to the conflict between me and the union in my last year at the institution which I [have] referred to earlier.

Figaji also commented on the mergers between the universities of Durban-Westville (UDW) and Natal, and the University of the Transkei and the technikons in the Eastern Cape. In his opinion:

UDW was seen as a weak institution because of the student unrest and ineffective leadership. The theory was that if you add it to Natal University, which was perceived to be strong, then both institutions would become strong. Instead they both got weakened and it took a long time for the merger to settle down.

An even more complicated merger was between the University of Transkei, Border Technikon and Eastern Cape Technikon. This was a three-institution merger of different institutional types and a few hundred kilometres apart, but collectively known as Walter Sisulu University (WSU). This merger was further plagued by bad leadership and consequently the VC was suspended and the Minister appointed an Administrator with the expressed instruction to propose the closure of the University. Fortunately, the Administrator returned to say that all WSU needed was better management. The sad part of this merger experiment is that no one has calculated the additional cost or evaluated the effectiveness of these decisions.

The human aspect that Figaji feels was important in his academic leadership becomes even clearer when he communicates about the staff meetings he had as VC of Pentech:

Once a year I had a meeting with all the staff ranging from gardeners to senior academics to give them an opportunity to ask any question on any matter affecting our institution. The meeting was also aimed at building a sense of an inclusive campus community. The staff used to ask questions about their pension fund's performance, new buildings being planned and a variety of other matters of interest. It was a very useful general engagement with staff. In the 2003 meeting, one of the secretaries said to me, "We understand you don't like the mergers, and you are planning to leave the institution when the merger takes place. Why are you deserting a sinking ship; leaving us orphans"? It affected me and I thought, maybe I should stay for at least a year after the merger and then leave at the end of 2005. During 2004, my last year, the conflict with the Union, referred to earlier, happened about the article they had written in which they claimed that I was "always dishonest". I had initiated the disciplinary action already when our annual staff meeting was due to take place. We had the meeting but this time it was not [a] question-and-answer [session], but rather I took the opportunity to make a statement to all the staff.

I recounted to the staff the request made to me at the previous meeting to stay on a little longer. However, given the statement made by the Union about me being dishonest, and the fact that the rest of the Union membership did not question the accuracy of this statement, I must assume that they all agreed with the statement. I concluded that if the staff believed this of me then I certainly could not, and would not, stay and I announced that I would leave on 31 December 2004.

After that, I had a Union delegation in my office claiming that they were not aware of this and that they were going to reverse this situation. They then started a petition on campus to try to get Union members to distance themselves from the position taken by the Union executive, but it was too late – I was not going to be convinced to stay.

Effective leadership and management

We asked Figaji what he found constituted effective leadership and management:

I think it is important as a leader to demonstrate that you respect your people and what they do; to delegate with a degree of confidence; to be firm and clear about what the rules of engagement are and what the measures of success are. Around any task, people want to know that their individual contribution is going to be valued, that they are part of a winning team. Your followers look to you for some sense of consistency; they must be able to anticipate how their leader will react in a certain situation. I think that, particularly in education leadership, the leader needs to be present. The leader needs to be present for both the students and staff. You cannot lead a South African institution from the plane, or from Europe or America, where you are spending half of your life at conferences. That cannot be done. If there is a weakness in our higher education leadership, I think it is a matter of "Where are you? How much time do you spend at your home base? How much time are you spending with the people who need your guidance?" Next, "Where are you spending your resources? Do you know what is spent on what?" I would say to a VC, "If you don't know where the last R50 000 was spent, you are out of touch". And all too often that is delegated to the extent that you have almost abdicated responsibility. By that I am not suggesting that you should be micromanaging. You must know how the budget has been allocated and that there is a system of accountability which is regularly monitored. The conversation between the Finance Department and the VC is as important as the conversation with the deans.

Unlike many of the other institutions, we managed the budget collectively at the centre as opposed to decentralising it. That was one of the big differences between Cape Technikon and Peninsula Technikon at the time of the merger. In a decentralised system faculties would say, "I have so many students, I generate so much from the state subsidy and I should get so much money". In a centralised system, such as the one at Pentech, we had an extended management team, which included all the deans and administration managers. We decided together what the general institutional costs were, like graduation and other common activities, and we top-sliced that cost. One of the things we did as a management team at the institution to encourage innovation and thinking out of the box, was to allocate one million rand per year to a faculty for innovation. This was included in the amount top-sliced from the budget. Then we split what remained between the academic and administration sectors in an agreed proportion and the responsible DVCs [deputy vice-chancellors] sat with their managers to allocate to departments and units within the institution.

Figaji's objection to the decentralised model of financial allocation was thus that it generated a competition for funds, and it hindered the kind of cross-subsidisation needed for either common or innovative projects across the University and did not foster a sense of community. We asked Figaji to expand on his notion of the centralised model:

Essentially, I believe that in a small institution you can create a much closer sense of community, and one of the ways of fostering this is to have a broader group of people participating in the decisions about the allocation of resources. The decision is not that of the VC only, but a more generally agreed-upon decision and direction.

By way of a practical example, I will expand on the way we dealt with staff appointments. Firstly, it is important to state that we never retrenched any staff, ever, at Pentech, because I could convince the senior managers that, when we appoint staff, we as the managers must be absolutely sure that we will need them well into the future, and that every appointment must be taken very seriously because it is about respect for the individual and the family she or he supports. We were very happy to deal with underperformers and dismiss them, but it was unacceptable for management to say we are going to discontinue this programme and, therefore, we would need to lay off people. Secondly, at any education institution the staff cost is the largest single budget item and, if not managed carefully, will soon create an unaffordable cost to the institution. We all agreed that the staff cost would not exceed a specified percentage of the total income of any given year.

In the middle of the year, departments and units would submit their applications for new staff for the following year to the responsible DVC, who would interrogate the application and, once satisfied, would submit it to Finance for costing. At the senior managers' meeting we would agree on the most likely anticipated total income and match the allowable expenditure on staff against the cost of the requests. In this way, we ensured that the institution did not make appointments it could not afford.

On one occasion, the state subsidy information was sent to us very late in the year and the amount was much lower than we had expected and we could not afford to make any new appointments and, even though posts had been advertised and some interviews conducted, I had to call together all those concerned and explain to them why we were not filling any new positions that year. There was great unhappiness, or rather disappointment, but they all understood the system and the logic. It is about consistency and fairness and the interest of institutional sustainability.

The centralised system also allowed us to get easy agreement on the need to provide properly for maintenance and the replacement of equipment, library books, vehicles and systems as they become obsolete. Often these items are neglected in the budget because of other financial pressures. We would top-slice a fixed percentage and hold this money separately under the headings mentioned above. These annually allocated amounts [would] either be used or [would] accumulate in the account for when needed. In this way, the cost of the maintenance of our buildings did not compete for resources with other items on the current budget. So any replacement of books, computers, machines or vehicles would be paid for from this fund and not from the annual budget allocation.

There are unfortunately some negative aspects of this approach which must be considered, but in general we found this to work for us by getting everyone to feel they have to be responsible financially. On one occasion, the Budget Controller in Finance came to me and said,

"This has been happening for two years now, from the fourteenth of September I get all these orders" – typical of government spending where there is wasteful expenditure at the end of the financial year because of surpluses. She pointed out that faculties had not used their money as agreed in the allocations, and now they were purchasing items that were not on the budget in order to clear the unspent allocations. This spending action was precipitated by the fact that the annual purchasing window closed at the end of September. This finance official felt sufficiently empowered to raise this matter with me and I had to take a hard line and stop this practice, which I did in a meeting with all the affected parties. That created some tension between me and my senior management, but it required an unpleasant decision to be made, and the leader must be willing to take those decisions.

We then asked Figaji what leadership qualities he thought a leader of an academic institution should possess:

There are always two sides to that coin. One side says you need a manager; the other one says you need an academic leader, somebody who is going to lead the research and teaching. Ideally you need a combination of those. But I would lean towards somebody who can manage the institution without being too managerial. I think there has got to be a respect for the academic endeavour, maximum support for the academic endeavour; there has got to be a recognition that the only reason we are here is because of what happens in the classroom. I think if that remains the focus of the leader at the institution and he [/she] manages his [/her] people and resources well, then that is the more complete person.

Pushing up the research outputs might be part of the job. I am not sure that the researchers want the VC to lead research and lead the research outputs. I think the leader needs to look after the institution, after its students, its staff and its resources so that everybody can do the job that they are paid to do. You must make sure that those jobs actually get done. I think that is the tough part.

We probed this view, and asked him what he thought the differences were between leadership and management in a university:

I think this question always generates a healthy debate. I am not sure it is actually worth spending the energy trying to dissect the difference. Clearly, management is about looking after the effectiveness and efficiency of the operation, and whether the system works; whereas the leader is visionary and gets people to willingly follow and support her or him to reach a particular goal. I think it is important for an institutional head to have fairly distinct leadership qualities, to be willing to engage with people and be able to convince people to follow. The reason I am so hung up on mutual respect is because I believe it is the central ingredient for good leadership. If one manages in a climate of mutual respect, then you draw the parameters that define your interaction. That is why I think there is such an interrelation between the two. If one manages the institution well, then you have passed the first hurdle. Then you need to produce the vision that people will agree to help you achieve.

In my own case, I had to convince all the staff, including gardeners and cleaners, that they should help me to make Peninsula Technikon the Massachusetts Institute of Technology (MIT) of Africa. The first time I said this to academic staff, they looked at me as if I had lost my mind. I spent many general staff meetings talking about [how] ... the MIT of Africa simply meant that we wanted to be known as the leading institution in technology and innovation in Africa, in much the same way as MIT is seen in the USA [United States of America]. This vision gave rise to the building of a new computer centre and a programme to ensure that every student was computer-literate and had access to the Internet. It resulted in the one million rand innovation fund for faculties and it resulted in many innovative technological applications on campus. These were quite novel issues at the time of the mid-nineties. I asked every department and unit to indicate how they would advance the vision of the MIT of Africa in their specific domains.

It is very important that the leader ensures that the signalling of a vision must be accompanied by resources, an implementation strategy and constant monitoring.

Figaji's concern about leadership in higher education was that there was not enough personal commitment to the job. The VC was not spending enough time among his or her people – both staff and students. This position leaves very little time for anything else.

Lessons learnt in local and international contexts of higher education

We asked Figaji what lessons he could share with us about being a leader in a university; what did he think were important lessons to share with others?

I have already signalled a few lessons but, as I look back, I probably think first of the things that I did not do. One of the things that worries me is that I was not proactive enough to help people prepare for their retirement. Institutions must talk to the forty-year-olds, or get someone to interact with them, to talk to them about what will happen to them when they reach 60. I served as a trustee on the pension fund to ensure that the investments made were beneficial and, in this context, I often gave staff feedback on the pension fund's progress, but I did not take the opportunity to help staff more broadly to prepare for retirement.

You always think you could have done better in a range of things. In retrospect, because we were a relatively small institution, we actually achieved quite a lot. For example, we created many opportunities for students and staff to advance. On one occasion, we negotiated an opportunity to send 15 students to Malaysia for in-service training; it was a huge event for these young people, many of whom had not experienced air travel before. I think that the important advice for a VC is walk the talk, get amongst your students, get amongst your staff, and get to know them in the larger university and not only in meetings.

Figaji has also worked internationally in higher education leadership and he shared with us what he learnt:

The one thing that I found very useful that the TELP Programme provided was the opportunity to identify a leader of a university in the USA that could help us with strategic planning. I chose the President of a University in Delaware, Dr William De Lauder, an outstanding individual who was humble, thoughtful and very experienced as a university leader in the USA. He came to South Africa once a year for an extended period of two to three weeks and would spend time with each of the senior leaders helping us as an institution with our strategic planning. I found it very valuable and helpful to have an external resource giving me feedback on how I was doing and how I could improve. This mentor soon became a family friend.

I think this could be a very valuable method of helping our current VCs to get to grips with their jobs. Unfortunately this method does require some humility from the VC.

The role of the Senate and Council

We asked Figaji about the role of the Senate and Council at Pentech during his period as VC:

I think we had a very strong Council; we had a council that, if you said to anyone in the Western Cape, the Chair of my Council is so and so, they would say, "Oh! Ok. That is good!" I always said to my colleagues that, if people cannot say that about the Chair of your institution's Council, you have the wrong Chair. We had significant business people in the Council; one year the head of the Stellenbosch Farmers' Winery; another, a head of Murray & Roberts; we had a judge; and we had the Chairman of BP; the head of our Finance Subcommittee was the head of Cape of Good Hope Bank. So we had significant people with recognisable skills in the Council, but, most importantly, they were all people who had achieved success in their professions – they did not need to enhance their CVs [curricula vitae] by serving on our Council.

We asked him how that came about:

Generally, the Council is made up of nominees from various sectors, so we would suggest to the sectors who we believed from their sector would be a good candidate and invariably they would nominate that person. Once we had these nominations I would approach the appropriate people to ask them if they would accept nomination for a particular position such as Chairperson or to lead the subcommittees. I would then ask individual members of Council if they would nominate specific people for specific positions, and I would explain what skill that person brings. It is very difficult to oppose the selection of the head of a bank as the Chair of the Finance Subcommittee unless there is another person with equal or better skills. The Council is too important a body to just leave to the whims of unaffected individuals in the nomination or selection process; it needs active managing. Appointing high-quality individuals also safeguards the sustainability of the institution and certainly will keep the institutional management on their toes all the time.

We expressed surprise that a VC of an institution could have such a determining role in the composition of the Council, and asked him whether this did not compromise its independence:

Even though I was so intimately involved in the composition of the Council, and they were generally very supportive of management, we did not have an easy ride at all. Let me illustrate this by way of examples. A local company was offering empowerment shares at a greatly reduced rate to qualifying individuals and organisations. I thought this was a wonderful opportunity for our institution to invest for a great return, and I was very excited and the next morning, in our usual meetings, I showed my management team my calculations which got them excited and we all agreed that we should invest. The Finance Director in the meeting agreed to make the arrangements for this acquisition. As I got to my office, it struck me that we were too hasty and did not consult the Council. I called the Chair of Finance who listened to me carefully and said that he would consult our asset managers and would get back to me. Thirty minutes later I got a call from the Chair of Finance turning down our scheme. I was disappointed, and a little angry, and tried to argue but soon realised that this was not going to change things, so we had to reverse the transaction.

On another occasion, I discovered that our Director of Finance had defrauded us of about one-and-a-half million rand. I was angry and disappointed but took all the steps to deal with the matter, including suspending the individual pending a hearing, attaching his pension and finding all the proof for a conviction. I proudly called the Council Exco together to report the matter and inform them of our action. Expecting to get some praise for the strong proactive action I took, the Exco reprimanded me for allowing this to happen and made it very clear that they expected me to recover all the money lost. I was deflated and felt unappreciated, but the lesson was clear; the ultimate responsibility was mine. Even though I [had] a strong hand in the composition of the Council, I knew that I could not overstep the mark, and, if they said no, that was the final word on the matter.

We asked Figaji if he thought something had changed in the way Council members are nominated in recent times. He explained that, in his view, the problem lies with the Ministry:

Previously, we would send a list of names to the Minister for him to nominate four people on a list of six, where we indicated each individual's strength and the skills they would bring to the Council. The Minister would appoint from the list we gave him with our recommendations. This was very helpful because it complemented the skills we had in the other nominees. This started to change with Minister Asmal and ... [he] nominated from outside that list, which was his prerogative to do, but unfortunately his intention was not to build the skills needed on Council but to ensure that he had people on Council who would support his merger ideas.

For example, during the merger process, when our Council was discussing whether we were going to take the Minister to court or not on the merger, one of his nominees was the one voice in Council who opposed it. I knew from behind the scenes that the Minister had spoken to her because he knew we were going to take him to court. So I asked the Chair to allow me to ask the Council member whether the Minister had spoken to her. She turned red, but denied it. But I knew the Minister had spoken to her... In the long term this is going to be detrimental to the institution.

One of the big battles I had on the Council was to ensure that my students and my staff behaved as Council members – that is, as representing the institution, not this or that constituency. Whenever one of the student members put their hands up and said, "Mr Chairperson, as students...", I would make a point of order. "You are not here as a student leader, but as a Council member in the interest of the institution and not your party or your student body. You are making decisions in the interests of the institution. You have to show your maturity as Council members." One time, I had to overrule a Union member in the Council who raised matters of Union interests. I said he undermined my role as the VC of the institution. If the Union had a concern, they should raise it with me as VC and I would bring it to Council if necessary. He was not the spokesman in the Council for the Union. If he was allowed to conduct himself in that way, Council would then have started to interact directly with the Union, which would not be their role at all. Unless there is a mature Council of intelligent people who understand their role, there will be interference. And part of the problem in my old institution is exactly that.

Post-1994: Ministries of education

Figaji was asked to reflect on his experience of the post-1994 changes in higher education:

I think it was very interesting for me personally, because I had quite a lot of interaction with the Minister and the planning for the transformation of higher education. At the time of the transition, I was the Chairperson of the Committee of Technikon Principals, and that brought me closer to the then Minister, Minister Bhengu. I had a close working relationship with the people who were in the Minister's office and the Minister's advisors. I served on the National Commission on Higher Education (NCHE) in 1997, so I was quite in tune with the things we were seeking to do.

Figaji commented that, while there were positive developments in the higher education sector, the schooling sector faced problems. Referring to ministerial management styles, he added:

Minister Asmal was interested in micromanagement. The one thing I must give Minister Asmal credit for was his decisiveness. He was not scared to make a decision. If you asked a question you knew you'd get a response. He was quite clear on many of the governance issues during a fairly difficult time.

However, Figaji felt that some of his decisions were made for political reasons rather than for the benefit of the sector. As Figaji was clearly very unhappy about the mergers, we asked him to explain:

I was not happy with the merger; not at all. I think it was the worst decision we ever made in the country. One of the issues that occupied the attention in the NCHE was the whole idea of diversification of higher education and the importance of offering diversified opportunities to students. Even in the technikon community, I did not support the view that technikons should change their names to universities. Instead, I suggested a compromise that would allow technikons to offer degrees; I supported that, because of the public recognition a degree would give a student. I argued within the Committee of Technikon Principals that we should focus on the degree-granting compromise as opposed to changing our institutional make-up and name. The initial move was only to have technikons offer bachelor's degrees and in exceptional cases master's degrees. Eventually permission was given, but it went to doctoral level. One of my arguments to limit the qualification level was that, as soon as we went to doctoral pro-grammes, it would change the fundamentals of what we were doing. If our main mission was technological advancement, then we have to focus on technological transfer, as opposed to getting into the business of esoteric research. Yet, if you offered doctoral programmes, that's where it pushed us to; that was my crude and basic argument. I did not win that one.

The technikons began to offer these higher degrees and it did help them in terms of reputation and acceptability. What we had in the country at this stage was further education and training (FET) colleges, technikons and the universities. The universities were well established and ranged from primarily teaching institutions to research-led institutions. The technikons were a new kind of institution and were growing; they were building a reputation focused on appropriate skills for a new economy and were becoming very successful. One good thing that Minister Pandor started, and Minister Nzimande accomplished, was to shift the FET colleges into the higher education sector. This brought more money and a greater focus to the colleges, and transformed the higher education landscape. Unfortunately, the mergers changed this landscape to only having FET colleges and universities, even though there is an attempt to distinguish between universities and universities of technology.

Figaji went on to explain why he opposed mergers so vehemently:

> The Minister [Asmal] had said to us, "I am going to change higher education so that it is unrecognisable. That is going to be my legacy, and people will remember me for that". We did not quite understand at that point what he was talking about. Although the Minster and I had our differences, we were also quite friendly toward each other before the merger debates. We had invited him to open our new IT [information technology] centre.
>
> When Minister Asmal proposed his merger plan, it was a difficult time in higher education; there were a lot of student protests and the institutional leadership was a serious problem. Bear in mind the country was then newly free, with Mr Mbeki now the President. All the exiles were returning home with good foreign qualifications and looking for senior positions. I can recount four or five institutions where VCs were parachuted in from the USA to head these institutions. They were all well qualified but they knew nothing about the South African higher education situation or the social dynamic within the country.

Figaji explained how the sector was faced with a problem where many of the historically black institutions faced leadership challenges and were not very stable:

> Some of the troubles were about leadership style; others simply mismanagement. Some of it was a failure to recognise that the black institutions had been centres of struggle and that one could not just switch students on and off, from one moment to the next, from struggle mode to peaceful mode.
>
> So, during the transition, the major portion of student protest action would emanate from the black institutions and this would taper off as we moved forward with our democracy. We had to accept that the black institutions were the sites of struggle during apartheid and would remain centres of struggle against whatever else presented itself as the new problem, and in some cases this new problem was inept institutional leadership. So the need to fix the leadership crisis at black institutions became of paramount importance. I argued that South Africa needed smaller institutions where it is possible to give

students who come with many disadvantages some personal attention so that their success provides the proof that education is the most powerful tool for liberation. To achieve this we needed to be bold and get the most appropriate leadership for our institutions given the fact that the students are now inward-looking and critical. The Minister reasoned very differently by believing that, if he took an institution with a perceived strong leader and merged it with an institution with a perceived weak leader, it would result in a stronger institution. This demonstrated the Minister's lack of experience in management and leadership.

However, for a policy change, the Minister was required by law to consult the CHE [Council on Higher Education]. So the Minister asked the CHE to give him advice, and the CHE put a committee together on which I sat. We proposed three levels of institutions, 'bedrock' – admittedly a bad name, which got us into trouble; 'multipurpose'; and 'research' universities. We said the key was that all of them should get the same funding. According to the plan, the 'bedrocks' would only teach at the undergraduate level and focus on eradicating the deficits in knowledge that many students came with; multipurpose institutions would teach at undergraduate and postgraduate levels; and 'research' institutions would teach but also do research. The important change here was that there would be dedicated teaching institutions that would give students the proper grounding and make up for the disadvantages that they came with originally. We wrote the report and at the end, at the last meeting, some members of the Committee wanted us to give examples so people would understand the models. I argued that that would only lead to misunderstanding. Institutional leaders would go to that page where their institution was used as an example and say, "No, no, no". So the report was produced and the last page had examples of the three categories and our thoughts on which institutions would fit where. The black institutions looked at this and saw they were the 'bedrock' institutions and all the white institutions were not. They cried 'racist', and threw their hands in the air! But it was also not what the Minister wanted.

So when the revolt came from the institutions, the Minister said, "I have asked for advice from the CHE, but I am not taking their advice. I am setting up my own committee". So he set up a committee and that Committee came up with the merger idea, because the Minister wanted mergers in any case. But I know from private discussions that they were designing the institutional mergers to address the institutional instability. They said the institutions in the Western Cape were all stable and doing very well, [and that] they should technically leave them alone. But the Minister said that, politically, he could not leave the Western Cape alone and merge everywhere else. So he had to do something in the Western Cape. I was a thorn in the flesh at that time, because at that time, I was very vocal about the mergers being the wrong solution to the perceived problem. Finally, the Minister announced that, in the Western Cape, he proposed to merge Pentech and UWC. The VC of UWC at the time was not opposed to the merger. I said to him that the entire idea of dealing with troubles in this way was wrong. So I wrote an article for the newspapers congratulating the Minister on merging the two black institutions in the Western Cape and leaving the former white institutions unaffected. The Minster realised his mistake, withdrew that proposal, and proposed to merge Pentech and Cape Tech instead. I had some public meetings on the campus, where [SASCO] members supported the merger; I suspect on the prompting from the Minister. They have since admitted to me that they had been wrong to follow the Minister's appeal to them.

We then asked Figaji what his view was about mergers in general. According to him, the challenge with the mergers started with ML Sultan and Natal technikons in Durban, when the two institutions requested a merger. He added that this made sense, since there was only a fence between the two technikons and they were the same sort of institution. However, the problem arose when they tried to merge totally different institutions, or institutions 300 kilometres apart. He explained that the Minister had to find a merger that everybody was happy with. Even the two technikons that were merged in the Western Cape, Figaji said, have not recovered from it, because the cultures of the two campuses were so different. When he objected to it the first time, the Minister told him not to worry about it. He had said:

> "Don't worry about it! You are the stronger leader. You can do at Cape Tech what you did at Pentech. Fix it!" I told the Minister that it was not his decision to make; that it needed to be made by the Councils. If he had sat down with the two Councils of Cape Tech and Pentech and said that he wanted to propose some change, there would have been a different discussion. We may not have agreed, but the respect for each other would be entrenched. To mix those two cultures was a huge issue. I knew how many years it took us at Pentech to develop a culture with our students. To now walk into a foreign institution and start that all over again was a challenge. The merger idea and the way it was handled displayed a lack of understanding of the fundamentals of institutional leadership and management.

In my view the merger programme was a complete disaster. The consequence of this is that we now have the universities, the universities of technology, and FET colleges. The programmes that the technikons ran are virtually disappearing; they have been swallowed and absorbed into the universities in some shape and form. I don't believe we have the diversity of access and opportunities in higher education that was the original intention.

The single most pressing concern, I believe, to be facing the higher education sector is the lack of empathetic leadership and strong management.

Conclusion

Having been at the helm of Pentech for ten years, we asked Figaji to tell us what aspects of his leadership he was most proud of. He replied that he was most proud of the fact that his leadership team were able to ensure that they created an environment for their students that signalled to them that they respected them as human beings. The residences would be respectable places to live in, and the facilities that they would use would be the best that the institution could provide, and would be a sign of the respect the institution had for its students and staff. Figaji personally saw to the development of a computer centre that would:

> ... ensure that every student was computer-literate, given the fact that Pentech drew a lot of their students from the most rural parts of the Eastern Cape. Students had a top-end walk-in facility, and, having access to these computers the students took to it like a duck to water. It was clearly something that they were hungry for. If they were to be a technological institute, they had to demonstrate that intent. The institution spent a lot of money on that centre, and the ongoing costs of renewal of computers. Upon completion, they had four floors of computer labs with programmes that assisted students to build their computer-literacy confidence. The centre was also largely run by students the institution employed as tutors.
>
> That is probably the achievement that I am most proud of.

In his last days as VC, he built a postgraduate residence. It was a single-room residence that was completely wired, and had little kitchen-ettes and the comforts of life befitting a postgraduate student. Students would only be granted a place if they deserved to be there, again tying respect to academic success and achievement.

chapter 5

Two tales of quality and equality

Chris Brink

Professor Brink was Rector and Vice-Chancellor (VC) of Stellenbosch University in South Africa from 2002, where he led a transformation agenda which attracted national and international attention. Earlier, he had served as Pro VC (Research) at the University of Wollongong in Australia. Before that, he was Professor and Head of the Department of Mathematics and Applied Mathematics at the University of Cape Town, where he also served as Coordinator of Strategic Planning. Other positions he held include a Senior Research Fellowship at the Australian National University in the 1980s, a brief spell in industry in the United States of America (USA), a sabbatical and other leave periods at Oxford University, and intermittent visits to many other European universities.

Professor Chris Brink is currently the VC of Newcastle University in the United Kingdom (UK), where he took office in 2007. He is a Board member of Universities UK (where he chairs the Student Policy Network), the Russell Group, and the N8 (the partnership of eight major research-intensive universities in the north of England, where he also served as Chairman). He is a member of the Advisory Committee on Leadership, Governance and Management of the Higher Education Funding Council for England. Previously, he served on the boards of the national Quality Assurance Agency, the national Equality Challenge Unit (also as Co-Chair), the North East Local Enterprise Partnership, Jisc, and various regional boards. During Professor Brink's tenure as VC, Newcastle University twice won the Times Higher Education national Leadership and Management Award.

Chris Brink was born, grew up, and went to school in a small town at the southern end of the Kalahari. He studied at (what was then) the Rand Afrikaans University, as well as Rhodes University, before winning an Elsie Ballot Scholarship to the University of Cambridge. He is a logician with a Cambridge PhD, an interdisciplinary DPhil, master's degrees in Philosophy and Mathematics, and a bachelor's degree in Computer Science.

His research areas include mathematics, logic, philosophy and computer science, and he has published in all these fields. Before moving into management, he held the prestigious "A"-rating of the National Research Foundation (NRF), which ranked him as one of South Africa's leading scientists. He is a Fellow of the Royal Society of South Africa.

Professor Chris Brink relates two case studies of change management in South African universities. One is about the University of Cape Town (UCT) in the 1990s, and the other is about Stellenbosch University (SU) in the 2000s. Both tales are about the creative tension between two imperatives: quality and equality. Both give a personal perspective.

University of Cape Town

My tale of UCT is set against the background of mathematics. To understand why this is relevant we have to go back to the early days of apartheid.

In June 1954, Dr Hendrik Verwoerd, having introduced into Parliament a piece of legislation called the Bantu Education Act, addressed the Senate as follows:

> The school must equip the Bantu to meet the demands which the economic life of South Africa will impose on him... There is no place for him in the European community above the level of certain forms of labour. Within his own community, however, all doors are open... Until now he has been subject to a school system which drew him away from his own community and misled him by showing him the green pastures of European society in which he is not allowed to graze... What is the use of teaching a Bantu child mathematics when it cannot use it in practice? ... That is absurd. Education is not, after all, something that hangs in the air. Education must train and teach people in accordance with their opportunities in life ... It is therefore necessary that native education should be controlled in such a way that it should be in accordance with the policies of the State.[1]

From Dr Verwoerd's point of view this probably looked very logical. Under apartheid, black people were never going to be allowed to do skilled jobs, or enter the 'green pastures of European society'. There

---

1   Harrison, D. (1981) *The White Tribe of Africa – South Africa in Perspective* (University of California Press: Berkeley), p.191.

was, therefore, no point in providing them with an education that would have made that possible. But it is not Dr Verwoerd's reasoning for which this speech is known. What reverberated through South African history were its consequences, which made 'Bantu education' a swear-word to black people.[2]

One particular phrase took on a life of its own: "What is the use of teaching a Bantu child mathematics?" asked Dr Verwoerd. Whether or not he intended it, his rhetorical question could easily be interpreted as implying that black people were generally not capable of doing mathematics anyway, thus adding insult to injury. Mathematics, there-fore, became a contentious subject, even a political one, with the teaching – or rather the non-teaching – of mathematics regarded as one of the tools of oppression employed by the apartheid regime.

All of this was very relevant at universities in South Africa during the early 1990s, when it became clear that there would be a move towards a democratic dispensation. The university landscape, we may recall, was a fragmented one, as might be expected after decades of 'separate development'. For the best part of a century, South African universities had already been differentiated by language. The colonial-origin, English-medium universities of Cape Town, Rhodes, the Witwatersrand and Natal had, by evolution and by design, their Afrikaans-medium counterparts at Stellenbosch, Potchefstroom, Pretoria and Bloemfon-tein. To these the Nationalist government had, in the 1960s, added two more. The Rand Afrikaans University (for 'Christian National Higher Education') in Johannesburg was intended to be a counterweight to the well-established University of the Witwatersrand, and the University of Port Elizabeth (with its fairly brief experiment in bilingualism) was likewise to be a counterweight to Rhodes University in the Eastern Cape.[3] In addition, however, the logic of apartheid dictated that there should also be universities for black people, in the 'homelands' which grand apartheid had designated as the places where they belonged according to ethnic classifications.

Thus, in apartheid-speak, there would be a University of Zululand (UNIZUL) for amaZulu, and a University of the Transkei (UNITRA) for amaXhosa, and a University of Bophuthatswana (UNIBO) for Batswana, and a University of Venda (UNIVEN) for VhaVenda, and so on. In addition, to be absolutely clear that everybody should be in his or her

---

2   For a recent and different interpretation by the Afrikaner historian Hermann Giliomee, see http://politicsweb.co.za/politicsweb/view/politicsweb/en/page-71619?oid =323686&sn=Detail&pid=71619. Accessed 7 August 2015.
3   I am an alumnus of the Rand Afrikaans University and of Rhodes University.

own box, the University of Durban-Westville (UDW) was for Indian students, and the University of the Western Cape (UWC was for (so-called) coloured students.[4]

The fragmentation of higher education originated with another piece of apartheid legislation, called the Extension of University Education Act of 1959. Like many other such Acts, the consequence was the opposite of what the title proclaimed. The consequence – soon duly accomplished – was to get black students out of white universities. The pretext was that black students, where in this case 'black' meant 'not white', would all have their own universities, neatly packaged into ethnic classifications. As the internal tensions and external pressures on apartheid mounted over time, the Nationalist government realised that it would be to their advantage if some homeland universities were seen to be doing well, but this never really materialised. The Verwoerdian reality was that the black universities, as long as they could only draw students coming out of Bantu education, were always going to be separate but were never going to be equal.

By the early 1990s, therefore, higher education in South Africa was very much a system of white privilege. This happened despite the persistent opposition of some universities, from the introduction of the Extension of University Education Act onward. As Harrison says:

> Once more the protests swelled. The University of the Witwatersrand pledged itself "to uphold the principle that a university is a place where men and women, without regard to race and colour are welcome to join in the acquisition and advancement of knowledge". In Cape Town three thousand demonstrated outside Parliament when the Bill came up, among them a recently retired Chief Justice of South Africa, the Chancellor of the University of Cape Town, his Principal, and Vice-Principal, many of his teaching staff and most of the students. Inside, the Minister told members that "the only possible inference is that this agitation is taking place under the influence of a leftist movement in our country".[5]

---

4   In South Africa, not only under apartheid but also to this day, 'coloured' is an official designation of ethnicity. The term 'coloured' does not, in South Africa, carry the connotations it would have in the UK or the USA. In particular, 'coloured' does not mean 'black'. At the time of writing (2014), government statistics took into account four racial classifications: African black, coloured, Indian/Asian and white. In Afrikaans, coloured people are usually called 'brown people', rather than 'mixed-race', and this is a term that has been adopted by many coloured people. During apartheid most coloured people were mother-tongue Afrikaans speakers, and UWC was originally established as an Afrikaans-medium university.

5   Harrison (1981) The White Tribe of Africa, p.193.

Later, after the student uprising in Soweto in 1976, UWC started moving away from Afrikaans, and, in the 1980s, under the inspirational leadership of Jakes Gerwel, declared itself the 'intellectual home of the left'. The apartheid government found resistance not only from the old English-medium universities, which they would have anticipated and discounted, but also from the very 'bush colleges' for which blacks were supposed to be grateful.

In this apartheid-induced maelstrom of higher education in the late 1980s and early 1990s, most academics were still trying to carry on as normal with the day job of research and teaching. But many were also beginning to think of a post-apartheid South Africa. And one thread of that thinking was about mathematics. It was clear that the country would, finally, need and want black scientists, engineers, accountants and other professionals of the kind Verwoerd had tried to prevent. It was also clear that the generation of young blacks who had been deprived of mathematics at school were not interested in hearing that they were underqualified for entering the study of mathematics at university. The Freedom Charter had promised that the doors of learning would be open to all; that was their demand, and that demand would have to be met.

UCT had been trying to prepare for this moment. The Academic Support Programme (ASP) was created specifically to cater for under-prepared students entering disciplines like science, engineering and accountancy, and had already branched out into various innovative ventures. For example, the Alternative Admissions Research Project (AARP) was designed specifically "to provide a means of access for educationally disadvantaged students whose school results do not necessarily reveal their potential to succeed in higher education".[6] The teaching of mathematics was central to much of the work of the ASP. Always the gatekeeper for science and engineering, mathematics could easily become an obstruction in what was already a bottleneck. But this was no moment to stand on the niceties of school-leaving results.

I was at that time (from 1991 onwards), Head of the Department of Mathematics at UCT, which was responsible for teaching all mathematics courses in the University, including the 'service courses' which were a compulsory part of the curricula in science, engineering and commerce. If black students were to graduate in those disciplines, they would first have to pass their mathematics modules. Conversely, if the Department of Mathematics could not train up more black students

---

6   AARP is still functioning at UCT.

to the requisite standard in mathematics, the University could not graduate them. This blunt reality taught me an important lesson about 'widening participation'; what matters, in terms of both quantity and quality, is not entry, but exit. What matters is not so much the standard at which students enter your department, but, more importantly, the standard they have attained when they leave.

Of course there are caveats and uncertainties, and any university teacher in mathematics will be familiar with most of them. Taking on underprepared students is a lot of work. It is a risk, particularly to the student, because, despite everybody's best efforts, they might fail, which is demoralising and expensive. It is a challenge, because many of the standard teaching methods just do not work. It is also a manifestation of the 'teacher's dilemma': if the students fail, you will be accused of poor teaching; if the students pass, you will be suspected of having dropped your standards.

Against this were two factors. One was the inescapable fact that something had to be done, and it could not be done by anybody else. The other was a growing realisation that the joy and inspiration of teaching outstandingly gifted and well-prepared students (of which UCT attracted plenty) had a counterpoint, which was the joy and satisfaction of opening doors to people who had the will to succeed but who had not had the opportunity. The task of a mathematics department, or a university, is not only to take straight-A students and turn them into straight-A graduates. It is also to add value to those who most need it. There is professional pride in performing both these functions.

Accordingly, during my 12 years in mathematics at UCT, we invented, borrowed, or experimented with virtually every manner of teaching mathematics to underprepared students which I have encountered anywhere since then (barring only the technological developments which came afterwards). The recruiters in the ASP scoured schools to find likely entrants to the University. We tried an extended degree programme, where the bachelor's degree would be spread over four years instead of three, with less pressure and more support in the first two years. We experimented with teaching 'ASP-students' in their own groups, which had the advantage of peer learning and the disadvantage of separation from the mainstream, as well as teaching them in a mix with everybody else, which had the advantage of diversity but piled yet more pressure on the lecturers.

The ASP morphed into an Academic Development Programme (ADP), to make the point that we should move beyond remediation. We mounted more, and more intensive, tutorials. We appointed some teaching-only staff in a mathematics department which prided itself on research.[7]

We made it clear that everybody was expected to pitch in, research or no research. We created a continuously staffed 'Maths Hot Seat', where any first-year student could wander in at any time and ask any question relating to their work. We set up a 'Quiet Room' for studying, which had only one rule: absolute quiet. We invented computer-generated individual tutorial tests. We tried open-book exams, supplementary exams, extended exam times, and fortnightly assessments. We realised that we had much in common with our sister Department of Applied Mathematics, and so did they, and so we voluntarily merged the two departments (in 1995), long before mergers became a top-down management tool. The Science Faculty, under the wise deanship of Cliff Moran, raised the profile of teaching through a Committee on Undergraduate Education in Science (CUES).[8] This made space for the science ADP programme to operate as a central faculty initiative, rather than being seen as an adjunct activity.

Then we got a bit more radical. We realised that, while there was a problem with mathematics, there was a much wider problem with numeracy – or rather, innumeracy. Many students entering the University to study in the humanities or social sciences might, through the neglects of Bantu education, not have had any kind of exposure to anything mathematical for years. These students, hopefully, would not only graduate but would be leaders in the new South Africa. However, many of them were practically innumerate. So we set up a Numeracy Centre. The Numeracy Centre, in which we collaborated with the Statistics Department, offered a credit-bearing, one-semester course in Effective Numeracy to students in the Faculties of Humanities and Social Sciences. Designing and teaching this course was a very satisfying thing to do, not least because it slaughtered so many holy cows.[9]

The entry criterion was the inverse of the usual: you had to show that you did not have a school-leaving mathematics qualification (to avoid anybody taking the course as a soft option). There were no lectures, no handbooks, and in a sense, no syllabus. Teaching consisted entirely of

---

7   The National Research Foundation (NRF) at that time, and still today, rated individual academics according to their research performance. The top rating is an A, which means 'world-leading researcher', and in the 1990s there were fewer than 50 of these A-rated researchers in the entire country, across all scientific disciplines. Five of them were in the Mathematics Department at UCT.

8   I was the first Chair of CUES.

9   See Brink, C. (1999) 'Effective numeracy' in *Proceedings of the Royal Society of South Africa*, 54(2), pp.247–256.

problem-solving. Students would sit around a table in groups of four, we would hand out a problem-sheet, and they would try to figure out some answers, by whatever means came to hand. Tutors would move between the tables to give help and suggestions as needed, but no more than was needed. Problems would typically come from a newspaper, or advertising, or some facet of daily life. For example, most newspapers would carry a table of currency conversion every day. So a typical problem would be: "As you can see, one US [United States] dollar is worth R5.67 today. What is one rand worth in dollars?" Of course the students could not do it, which is why they were at the Numeracy Centre, so we had to learn to deconstruct a problem down to the very basics. "Suppose a dollar would buy you two rand. Then what would one rand be worth in dollars? And how did you get to that answer?"

We always encouraged students to use calculators, and they liked to do so, but they did not always know what the calculator was doing. To understand why the button labelled x^{-1} was the right one to use to calculate what R5.67 is worth in dollars was a revelation. Once some confidence had been gained, we moved on to teaching numeracy via spreadsheets. This gave the students some understanding of data, graphs and charts, and some computer proficiency, which they liked. At the same time, it gave us a platform to inculcate some understanding of the arithmetic behind spreadsheet manipulation.

The one piece of orthodoxy that we stuck to was that, at the end of the semester, students had to take an exam, and they had to do the exam individually. However, the exam had no time limit. Students would come in at nine o'clock, get their exam problem-sheet, sit down at a computer, and work away as long as they wanted – some brought their lunch. It was also open-book. They could bring any books, notes, other material, calculator or laptop they wanted. They could talk, but not confer. In the end, the exam was marked and graded just like any other, and the student would get a credit for the Effective Numeracy module, just like any other.

Both in Academic Support and in Effective Numeracy we learnt that there was no silver-bullet solution, and no quick fix. We tried everything we could think of, and some things worked for some students and other things worked for other students, and sometimes nothing seemed to work. But, on the whole, and over time, we made a contribution, and it was a worthwhile and satisfying thing to do.

These developments also played out on a bigger scale within the University as a whole. In 1996, the Senate voted, by the requisite two-thirds majority, to install Dr Mamphela Ramphele as the new Vice-Chancellor (VC) of UCT – the first black woman to head up a university in South Africa. She had made it clear to her colleagues that, if we wanted her to be VC, she would do it, but only on the understanding that she would make fundamental changes to the University, which, once appointed, she proceeded to do. I served for some while as the university-wide Coordinator of Strategic Planning, and by a VC edict, I was for that time made an ex officio member of every single committee and working group at the University. We restructured the faculties (from 11 to six). We reworked the curriculum (from subjects into programmes). I drafted the new mission statement, for a 'world-class African university'. That mission statement included some of the lessons learnt from mathematics, such as the principle of being 'flexible on access, but firm on success'. We invented a new structure, called the Centre for Higher Education Development (CHED), which was a 'horizontal faculty' lying at the base of the six vertical pillars representing the subject-based faculties and bringing together a number of initiatives such as the ADP.[10] CHED eventually also absorbed the Numeracy Centre, and both structures still exist.[11] All of this was happening at the same time as the post-apartheid changes in higher education driven at government level.

I left Cape Town at the beginning of 1999 to go to Australia, but I returned to South Africa three years later to become Rector and VC of Stellenbosch University.

Stellenbosch University

The Dutch Governor, Simon van der Stel, venturing into the interior from the Fort in Cape Town in 1679, was so enchanted with a pleasant wooded area on the banks of the Eersterivier (the 'first river') that he founded a settlement there and, somewhat immodestly, named it after himself. The town of Stellenbosch is in a beautifully scenic setting, and is a popular tourist destination, being also at the centre of the Western Cape wine route. It is well known amongst rugby fans as the base of a renowned club which has produced many Springboks for the national rugby team.

---

10 If you visualise CHED as a set of steps at the base of six pillars, and you put a triangular apex on top of those pillars to represent Admin/Management, you get a picture that looks uncannily like the front of Jameson Hall, the great hall of the University of Cape Town at the centre of the campus. Accordingly, the new model of six faculties plus CHED was known as the Jameson Hall model. (This greatly confused an international advisor on university restructuring, who went searching through the literature for two experts called Jameson and Hall.)

11 For CHED see http://www.ched.uct.ac.za/. Accessed 7 August 2015; for the Numeracy Centre, see http://www.numeracycentre.uct.ac.za/. Accessed 7 August 2015.

Less well-known is a fact that is also less pleasant. Stellenbosch was the birthplace and intellectual home of apartheid.

Stellenbosch University was created by the Afrikaners, for the Afrikaners. It was their beacon of hope during the slow but grimly determined climb back into power after the defeat of the Anglo-Boer War (which in my youth was still spoken of by my grandmother as 'the English war'). This drive for dominance took place from 1902, when the two Boer republics accepted defeat, through to 1910, when the Union of South Africa was founded, through two world wars, and through the Great Depression and the 'poor white' problem of the 1930s, until 1948. That was when the National Party of D.F. Malan, a former 'dominee' of the Dutch Reformed Church, defeated the United Party of Jan Smuts in a general election, winning the majority of seats in Parliament, although not the majority of the overall vote.

In the rise of Afrikanerdom to political power, Stellenbosch, and Stellenbosch University, played a considerable part. It was at Stellenbosch that the National Party was founded (in 1914, two years after the founding of its eventual nemesis, the African National Congress). It was at Stellenbosch that some of the great Afrikaner businesses were founded, such as the insurance giant SANLAM (Suid-Afrikaanse Nasionale Lewens-Assuransie Maatskappy) and the Afrikaans newspaper company Nasionale Pers (now a global communications company renamed Naspers). It was here, also, that the institution which had previously existed as Victoria College became, in 1918, the University of Stellenbosch, dedicated to Afrikaans and Afrikanerdom. Deep within the psyche of Stellenbosch is the story of how the University's founding was made possible by the bequest of £100 000 in the will of 'Oom Jannie' J.H. Hofmeyr, on condition that the money be used to ensure that Afrikaans would have 'geen mindere plaatz' – no lesser place – at the University than English. That is why, at the centre of Stellenbosch University campus, you will find the statue of J.H. Hofmeyr, with the simple inscription 'Ons Weldoener' – Our Benefactor. And that is why the issue of Afrikaans has been so prominent at Stellenbosch.

Surely it is one of the tragedies of the 20th century that the Afrikaners, who had the sympathy of the world after the Boer War, a strong case for self-determination, and the fortitude to overcome any adversity, went on to turn goodwill into animosity because they could not see any route to survival other than through power and domination. And surely, within that narrative, we should take account of how and why a university became the standard-bearer for a narrow ethnic nationalism, proclaiming itself as the 'white Athens of the South'.

For most of the 20th century, the power brokers of apartheid were Stellenbosch men. D.F. Malan was a Stellenbosch resident. Hendrik Verwoerd, before he went into politics, was a Professor of Sociology at Stellenbosch University. When Verwoerd was assassinated in 1966, the National Party appointed as his successor John Vorster, Minister of Police, who had in his youth been President of the Students' Representative Council (SRC), and eventually became Chancellor of Stellenbosch University. Vorster's brother, Koot Vorster, was the Moderator of the Dutch Reformed Church, which is sometimes referred to as the 'National Party at prayer'. Koot's colleague, 'dominee' Kosie Gericke, served as Chairman of the Council and Vice-Chancellor of Stellenbosch University (this position then being distinct from the position of Rector). Vorster's successor as Prime Minister, the formidable P.W. Botha, also became Chancellor of Stellenbosch University. Most of the rectors of Stellenbosch University were leading figures in the 'Broederbond', the secret organisation behind the National Party. H.B. Thom, Rector during the 1960s and one-time leader of the Broederbond, declared Stellenbosch to be the 'Volksuniversiteit' of the Afrikaners.

In a generous mood, one might say that, during apartheid, the Afrikaners wanted to give to black people exactly what they had so intensely desired for themselves – an ethnic university – hence the idea of a University of Zululand for the Zulus, a University of Venda for the Vendas, and so on. But the idea went wrong because the gift was unwanted. Most Afrikaners of the 20th century did not agree with, nor wished to explore, "the principle that a university is a place where men and women, without regard to race and colour [or indeed other markers of group identity] are welcome to join in the acquisition and advancement of knowledge".[12] Instead, mainstream Afrikaner thinking considered a university as a manifestation of group identity. Therein lay the difference with the liberal tradition, and the basis of the university's leading role in apartheid.

When I arrived in Stellenbosch from Australia in January 2002, I was only the seventh Rector since 1918. I was the first Rector to be appointed from outside the university, the first who was not an alumnus, and the first who had never been a member of the 'Broederbond' or any of the Afrikaner cultural organisations. I took office eight years after the democratic elections of 1994, when the new South Africa came into being. By coincidence, eight years was also the time between the Union of South Africa – the 'new South Africa' of that time – and the founding of the University. The time was therefore propitious for new thinking

---

12 Harrison (1981) *The White Tribe of Africa*, p.193.

about the nature and role of Stellenbosch. The story of how this new role was articulated, and how it unfolded, is told in a valedictory volume titled *Anatomy of a Transformer*, and in what follows I largely draw from there.[13]

How, I wondered, does a university which had been in the forefront of apartheid become an integral part of the new multiracial South Africa? This was a specific version of a fundamental question which has taxed anybody engaged in change management: how do you change a mindset? Many Afrikaners of the 20th century grew up in an apparently well-ordered world, in which God had authority over man, men had authority over women, older people had authority over younger people, and whites had authority over blacks. With a few notable and heroic exceptions, this world view was unchallenged from within, especially if you grew up on the 'platteland' (literally, the 'flat country', meaning the rural areas).

You listened to South African Broadcasting Corporation (SABC) radio, read *Die Burger*, and went to a Calvinist church, and these were the voices that informed your understanding of the world. I myself was an adult before I conducted a conversation in English, or read an opposition newspaper, or saw a television set. Much later, when I took up office as Rector and VC, I was conscious that many of the staff and most of the alumni of Stellenbosch University were, like me, apartheid's children. All the more reason, I felt, to engage with the new South Africa.

The first lever of change was to get academic buy-in for a different approach. This took shape in a statement called Vision 2012, in which the University committed itself to an outward-oriented role in South Africa, Africa, and globally:

Stellenbosch University:
a) is an academic institution of excellence and a respected knowledge partner,
b) contributes towards building the scientific, technological, and intellectual capacity of Africa,
c) is an active role-player in the development of the South African society,
d) has a campus culture that welcomes a diversity of people and ideas,
e) promotes Afrikaans as a language of teaching and science in a multilingual context.[14]

---

13 Botha, A. (ed) (2007) *Chris Brink: Anatomy of a Transformer* (SUN Press: Stellenbosch). Available from: http://www.africansunmedia.co.za/.
14 http://www.sun.ac.za/english/policy/Documents/Quality%20Development%20 Plan.pdf. Accessed 29 July 2015.

This five-point statement started turning the ship. It pointed the academic compass towards quality, but stood Verwoerdian ideology on its head by positioning diversity as an opportunity for increasing quality rather than a risk of losing it. It challenged the University to engage with the new South Africa, rather than keeping its head below the parapet, as it had done since 1994. It recognised and celebrated Afrikaans-ness, but in the context of a society which now had 11 official languages.

Actions, however, would speak louder than words. And so, in December 2002, Stellenbosch University became the venue for the quadrennial conference of the African National Congress (ANC). This week-long event was attended by thousands of delegates, with white faces the exception. To organise a conference on this scale you need facilities: transport, accommodation, catering, at least one very large auditorium, plenty of seminar rooms and breakout spaces. Stellenbosch University campus could provide all of these. Here was an event which could be seen as closing a circle of history: the new black rulers of South Africa would have their plenary session in the D.F. Malan Hall at Stellenbosch University. The conference was diversity made manifest, up close and personal. Rarely, if ever, had Stellenbosch seen black people (as in 'African black'), other than cleaners or builders, setting foot in the student halls of residence, let alone sleeping in the beds, or – in another reversal of an apartheid obsession – using the toilets. It took some interesting discussions inside the University to get to the point of signing the contract with the ANC. One member of the Estates staff encapsulated the anguish felt by many in a single remark: "But Professor," he said, "they will walk on the grass!"

Diversity needed to be followed by quality, and so we spent a lot of time and effort on raising academic performance. This was another one of the many ironies of that time and that place. To many Afrikaners, especially amongst the older alumni, Stellenbosch was literally peerless, because it was so much more than just a university. This led, over time, to a self-perception of excellence which was, unfortunately, more a reflection of the cultural insularity of the Afrikaner world than a realistic measure of the academic quality of the institution. Moves towards increasing diversity, therefore, routinely invoked suspicion and distrust from the wider Afrikaner community, with many refrains of the 'standards will drop' variety. Fortunately, most academics under-stood the matter rather better. The fact is that Stellenbosch had to work really hard to get into the same kind of academic ballpark as UCT and the University of the Witwatersrand (Wits). The University started doing so from around the mid-1980s, when national research metrics first appeared. This was a process I was glad to inherit from my predecessors, and pleased to support, and it worked. By 2006, the Deputy Vice-Chancellor (DVC) for Research could report that Stellenbosch produced more research publications and delivered more doctoral degrees per academic than any other university in the country, was joint first with UCT on papers in the Thomson Reuters *Science citation index*, first overall on weighted research outputs, and had bagged three of the first seven National Centres of Excellence and four of the first 15 National Research Chairs. The Business School had gained triple accreditation.[15] The new National Centre for Theoretical Physics was to be located at Stellenbosch. We had won an award as 'Technologically Most Innovative University in South Africa'. Also, with a large grant from the Wallenberg Foundation in Sweden, we had established the Stellenbosch Institute for Advanced Study (STIAS) – the first such venture in Africa.[16]

All of these quality improvements took place in parallel with a concerted recruitment effort to raise the student-diversity profile. Over a period of five years we raised the representation of coloured, black African and Indian students at Stellenbosch University by 70 per cent in terms of numbers, and from 19.7 per cent of the total student population to 28.3 per cent. The table on the facing page shows the growth curve.

In so far as comparisons can be drawn, these numbers would indicate a South African equivalent of what in the United Kingdom (UK) is called 'fair access' – the idea that a good university should make a conscious effort to recruit, fund, educate and graduate a substantial number of students from disadvantaged backgrounds. The comparison should be treated with caution, because 'black' does not necessarily equate to 'disadvantaged'. Indeed, it would be tragic if the new South Africa cannot over time invalidate such an equation. Nonetheless, in the first decade of the 21st century, the legacy issues of apartheid were still so prevalent that, by and large, black students came from less affluent households than white students (and, in some cases, from poverty-stricken households, or from no households at all).

---

15 'Triple accreditation' is a sought-after accolade amongst business schools. It means being accredited simultaneously and independently by EQUIS (the European Quality Improvement System), AMBA (the Association of MBAs), and AACSB (the Association to Advance Collegiate Schools of Business).
16 Brink, C. (2007) 'The state of the university' in Botha, *Anatomy of a Transformer*, pp.29–30; for the Stellenbosch Institute for Advanced Study see www.stias.ac.za. Accessed 7 August 2015.

Stellenbosch University contact education students by level of study and race for 2001 to 2006[17]

YEAR	2001	2002	2003	2004	2005	2006
Undergraduate (headcount)	12 228	12 698	13 416	13 446	13 863	14 173
By race						
White	10 525	10 704	10 947	10 909	11 088	11 167
Coloured	1 346	1 518	1 776	1 890	2 036	2 195
Black	234	336	504	471	550	617
Indian	123	140	189	176	189	194
Percentage coloured, black & Indian	13.9%	15.7%	18.4%	18.9%	20.0%	21.2%
Postgraduate (headcount)	6 031	6 160	6 341	6 857	7 244	7 420
By race						
White	4 132	4 091	4 124	4 172	4 213	4 315
Coloured	663	656	662	860	1 017	1 042
Black	1 050	1 160	1 289	1 586	1 782	1 838
Indian	186	253	266	239	232	225
Percentage coloured, black & Indian	31.5%	33.6%	35.0%	39.2%	41.8%	41.8%
All students (headcount)	18 259	18 858	19 757	20 303	21 107	21 593
By race						
White	14 657	14 795	15 071	15 081	15 301	15 482
Coloured	2 009	2 174	2 438	2 750	3 053	3 237
Black	1 284	1 496	1 793	2 057	2 332	2 455
Indian	309	393	455	415	421	419
Percentage coloured, black & Indian	19.7%	21.5%	23.7%	25.7%	27.5%	28.3%

We, therefore, needed to reset the quality indicators for students. The standard indicators of "what were your school-leaving grades?" or "what school did you come from?" would clearly work against the disadvantaged, and in favour of those who entered exuding the fragrance of advantage. As I had learnt at UCT, exceptionalism would also not work. To treat disadvantaged students as an identifiable cohort to whom different standards and measures apply would be to stigmatise them as inferiors who need to be tolerated, rather than challengers who should be welcomed. While 'disadvantaged' was still visibly manifested as 'not white', such separation would confirm rather than overturn the prejudices of apartheid.

The fact of the matter was that many of the black students we admitted had faced hardships that students with the advantage of stable middle-class or affluent homes could not imagine, and might not have been able to overcome. Advantage creates opportunity, and can buy

---

17 Special students excluded.

the preparation necessary to make the most of it. Conversely, disadvantage entails fewer opportunities and less ability to exploit them when they do arise. It is no use the doors of learning being open when the edifice itself is at the top of a mountain you cannot climb.

What we had to do at Stellenbosch was to change the mindset about what quality means. One new initiative that helped to do so was an award I instituted, called the 'Rektor se Uitstygtoekenning' – literally, the 'Rector's Rise-Up Award', which became known in English as the 'VC's Award for succeeding against the odds'. This was a large cash award, double a normal full-cost bursary. The University already had the usual kinds of awards for attainment, including the very prestigious annual Chancellor's Medal for the graduate with the highest level of academic achievement. The Rise-Up Award was different. It gave recognition not to a number, but to a story. The question was not what grades you had attained, either at school or at university. Your grades had to be good enough to get you into university, or to pass your exams, but this was not the determining factor. What qualified you for an award was the distance you had travelled, and the obstacles you had had to overcome, to reach your level of attainment. In short, the Rise-Up Award was based on a value-added understanding of quality: performance seen against context. When opportunity is not equally available to all, then merit cannot just be a number. The narrative should also come into consideration.

Besides the money, and the conceptual clarity of the scheme, we also had to make sure that it enjoyed esteem. For that purpose we used the annual opening of the academic year, which at Stellenbosch is a formal event where the VC delivers an address to the student community, including the entire intake of new students, in the company of senior academic staff. We endowed this event with the same kind of academic pomp and circumstance as would normally be used for a graduation ceremony, and we treated the Rise-Up awardees in the manner usually reserved for honorary graduates. The event started with an academic procession, in full academic dress, and was presided over by either the Chancellor or the VC. There would be words of welcome, in particular to the new students, followed by the VC's address. The main moments of the ceremony, though, would be the presentation of the Rise-Up Awards. Each awardee would be asked to step forward onto the podium, and the University Orator would deliver an address essentially consisting of a short biography of their life and circumstances, and how, despite those circumstances, they had nevertheless managed to pursue successful academic studies. It was never necessary to 'big' it up. The stories were, without exception, absolutely compelling, and, to many of the young white Afrikaners in the audience, an absolute revelation. And not only to them, but also to many academics.

At the first awards ceremony, I put the matter thus:

> In line with our Vision Statement, Stellenbosch University strives to be an academic institution of excellence, with a national profile and an international reputation. Quality must be our benchmark. If so, we have to ask a simple but profound question: how do you judge quality relative to context? Some of us take for granted an environment which for others is only a dream. If so, is it not the case that our performance, no matter how well merited on the basis of our own efforts, also owes something to the environment within which we live and work?
>
> Consider two hypothetical cases. One is a student whose parents are well-educated professional people, reasonably affluent, and who comes to us from one of the so-called 'good schools', where she enjoyed every possible facility for sharpening the mind. The other is a student whose parents have had little formal education and who live in poverty, who comes to us from a historically disadvantaged school in a gang-infested area. If the former student comes to Stellenbosch with a school-leaving mark of 90 per cent, and the latter comes with a school-leaving mark of 70 per cent, is it possible for us to say that the former is a better student than the latter? And if we do, would that be right?[18]

Here is an example: the case of Ella Davids – not her real name, but a true story. She grew up in a deprived area of the 'platteland', where coloured people are mostly agricultural labourers, went to a small rural school, under circumstances she described as 'frustrating', and matriculated with results which, on the numbers alone, would seem fairly mediocre. "My childhood dreams and aspirations faded away", she said later, "and I swore never again to read a book or learn something." After leaving school, she worked for a number of years as a fruit packer, in a grocery store, and as a nanny. Gradually, however, her dream of going to university was rekindled, in part through her involvement with a church group. Ten years after leaving school she plucked up the courage to go and see the local 'dominee'. The 'dominee' called a friend of his at Stellenbosch University, and a remarkable chain of events was set in motion. Two weeks later, Ella arrived in Stellenbosch with R200 in her pocket "and a word from the Lord". She was 28 years old. She found accommodation in a backyard in Cloetesville, a coloured neighbourhood of Stellenbosch, enrolled for a degree in theology,

---

18 Botha, *Anatomy of a Transformer*, pp.5–6.

and walked to campus every day. By the end of that academic year she had completed 13 semester courses, nine of them with distinction, including Greek I with a final result of 98 per cent. In her second year, her results were not quite as impressive because she had had to take on a job to support herself. Nonetheless, she once again passed most of her subjects with distinction, including Greek II with 94 per cent. The Rise-Up Award, which Ella won at the end of her second year, enabled her to realise her potential without the pressures of financial hardship. She later completed her master's degree with distinction, and was working on her doctoral dissertation by the time I left Stellenbosch.

The Rise-Up Award brought to the fore many stories of succeeding against the odds. There was the black student who grew up in a corrugated-iron shed in Khayelitsha in the troubled 1980s, wrote matric under the muzzles of police guns, stole train rides to get to the UWC, and ended up with a PhD in Physics from Stellenbosch University. There was the quadriplegic who went from Stellenbosch to the University of Oxford. There was the young woman who lost her handicapped father shortly after leaving school, and found herself at the age of 20 as the head of a household with a handicapped mother and a handicapped sister, both unemployed, who nonetheless came to Stellenbosch and completed her degree with distinction.

Nobody can deny the merit of these students. But conventional means of admission and reward might not have picked them up, because, when attainment is viewed without regard to context, others would at some crucial stage have outshone them, and without support the exigencies of their circumstances might have killed off any chance of success.

Part of change management is about finding allies, and I was fortunate in having the best kind of critical collegiality from a number of the leading academics of Stellenbosch.[19] Amongst Stellenbosch academics there had long been a numerically small, but symbolically large, number of outsider–insider academics who spoke out against apartheid and its consequences – people like the theologian Bennie Keet, the philosophers Johan Degenaar and Willie Esterhuyse, and the economist Sampie Terreblanche. This gave rise to what another philosopher, Anton van Niekerk, has called a 'second line' of thinking at Stellenbosch, against the Malan-Verwoerd-Thom-Vorster-Gericke line. Much of what we accomplished during my time at Stellenbosch

---

19 All the opinions expressed in this article are entirely my own, and are not in any way intended to represent the views of anybody mentioned by name.

would not have been possible without the precedent of this second line of thinking, and the active support of its descendants.[20]

I was also grateful to find two institutional change agents that I would never have anticipated: the Faculty of Theology and the Faculty of Military Sciences. By the time I arrived at Stellenbosch, the Faculty of Theology had undergone a complete mindset change from the days of the National Party at prayer. They had deeply engaged with their own past, had come to revere the thought leaders their church rejected in the apartheid days (Beyers Naude being a notable example), and were a constant and steady example of not complaining about the present nor fearing the future. They were by far the smallest faculty in the University, and on any organisational or financial analysis they really should not have existed as a separate faculty at all, but such was their value that I was more than pleased to give them every support.

The Faculty of Military Sciences, which was the academic face of the Military Academy of South Africa, had undergone an equally remarkable transformation from the days it only educated young white men for the old apartheid Defence Force. After 1994, in an extraordinary fusion, that body was merged not only with the various liberation movements such as Umkhonto we Sizwe (MK), but also the various homeland forces. One player in that process was Brigadier General Solly Mollo, who at the time I arrived at Stellenbosch was the Commandant of the Military Academy. Solly Mollo understood what the new Rector was trying to do, and he made an early symbolic gesture of support. For my first academic opening of the University, he brought the entire student body of the Military Academy in buses from Saldanha to the D.F. Malan Hall. I well remember getting goose pimples when that block of young men and women, black, coloured, white and Indian, arose in full military uniform, in what was otherwise a sea of white faces, stood to attention, saluted, and sang in full voice all four verses of the national anthem.

Finally, I should give some attention to the issue of Afrikaans at Stellenbosch, although the matter is complicated and probably deserves a longer narrative. If you were to go through old newspaper clippings of *Die Burger*, you might well think that the 'taaldebat', which was the debate about the role and function of Afrikaans at the University, was the defining feature of my tenure at Stellenbosch. My view is different. For me, the main issue of change management during my time at

---

20 I owe a personal debt for their friendship and support to Willie Esterhuyse, who first taught me logic, and Annemarie Esterhuyse, with whom I first taught mathematics.

Stellenbosch was about the concept of ownership. My speech at a rather fraught meeting of the Convocation in November 2004 summarised a number of debates in one key question: "Whose place is this?"

That question went back to one of those small incidents, which, in retrospect, can be recognised as a defining moment. Shortly after arriving at Stellenbosch, but long enough after for my views about the need for change at Stellenbosch to be public knowledge, my wife and I were guests at a Stellenbosch function where many alumni and stakeholders were present. Our host welcomed the new Rector of the University, and acknowledged his many plans and ideas, but did add one little word of advice. "Just remember, Professor," he said, "this is *our* place."

On this point, too, my view was different. I could not see Stellenbosch developing to its full potential as a contributor to South Africa, nor as an academic institution on the world stage, while it remained 'the place' of only one section of the rainbow nation. Such a characterisation would be contrary to Vision 2012. It would also go against the principle of a university having an open door for all those with the necessary ability to join in the acquisition and advancement of knowledge.[21]

It was fairly clear, despite the protestations of some diehards, that Stellenbosch could not be a place for the Afrikaners alone. But it was quite a subtle argument to make that, since the power base of Afrikaans-speakers lay with white Afrikaners, the idea of Stellenbosch as an Afrikaans university should be balanced against the risk of Stellenbosch actually remaining an Afrikaner university, with only a token presence of some Afrikaans-speaking coloureds, Indians or blacks.

I went to Stellenbosch with high hopes for the concept of an Afrikaans university. There is a strong argument for language diversity in a multicultural society and a clear historical case for Stellenbosch exercising leadership and taking responsibility for the promotion of Afrikaans. It seemed to me entirely feasible and desirable for Stellenbosch University to pursue such a goal, at the same time as striving for a more inclusive South African-ness. I even wrote a monograph about

---

21 I have expounded the idea of a world-class civic university – one that has both high academic output and functions in service to society. But, then, 'society' is not limited to one place, or one sector, and the university is not seen as the property of any particular community. A world-class civic university can have a strong sense of place and culture – but it should always have its eye on global society and global challenges, and it must always remain autonomous. Such a university will not allow a community to claim ownership over it, just as it will not allow the state or big business to claim ownership over it. At most, and insofar as the concept of ownership is applicable at all, a world-class civic university belongs to the academic body.

it, titled *No Lesser Place*.[22] Only as time went on did I – perhaps belatedly – realise that my concept of an Afrikaans university was fundamentally different from the concept of those who said, "this is *our* place".

My view of an Afrikaans university was that it is in the first place a *university*, and that whatever may be done or decided concerning Afrikaans would take place in the context of what is best for the academic profile of the university. Under this model, the promotion of Afrikaans is a strategic goal of the university, but not the only goal, nor the most important one. In the decision-making processes of the university, the promotion of Afrikaans would be in somewhat the same position as the goal of community engagement: an integral but not a dominant influence, and one that is derived from the academic life of the university. This academic model not only allows for, but actually requires, policy, procedures and structures to promote Afrikaans, in the same way and to the same extent as other strategic goals have such requirements.

The other view of an Afrikaans university was that it is in the first place *Afrikaans*, and whatever may be done or decided concerning academic matters would take place in the context of what is best for Afrikaans. According to this view, the first and foremost task of the university, is not the creation or dissemination of knowledge, but to serve as an instrument for the protection and retention of Afrikaans as a 'high-functioning' language. At Stellenbosch, this model manifested itself in a particular form, namely that the academic business of the University is in service of the identity of the people who work and study there, or have worked or studied or been associated with it in the past. Under such a premise, the University should act as guardian and gatekeeper, ensuring that only Afrikaans-speakers determine the direction, functioning and future of the University, and that academic business should be subservient to the perceived requirements of Afrikaans.

While not articulated in these terms at the time, in retrospect it became clear to me that it was the fundamental difference between the academic model and the identity model of an Afrikaans university that gave rise to a few years of 'taalstryd' (language battle) about the future of Stellenbosch University.

By and large the academics at Stellenbosch were, as I would have hoped, in favour of an academic model. To protect the development of that preference, however, I sometimes had to draw the fire of the

---

22 Brink, C. (2006) *No Lesser Place – the Taaldebat at Stellenbosch* (SUN Press: Stellenbosch). Available from: http://www.africansunmedia.co.za/.

'taalstryders' upon myself. Such had been the tradition in Afrikaner-dom of levels of authority that any decision by the University was, at any rate, easily assumed to have been at the command of the Rector. This happened, for example, with something called the T-option. The language policy of the University, which was formulated (by academics, for academics) during my first year in office, distinguished four language options for taught courses. The A-option was to teach in Afrikaans only. The E-option was to teach in English only. The A&E option was parallel-medium teaching – offering a module or course in full in both Afrikaans and English versions, which meant doubling up the effort. And the T-option was a licence to use both English and Afrikaans, at the discretion of the lecturer, within one course, and even within one class, without doubling up.

The Humanities Faculty rather liked the T-option, and after a year or two their Faculty Board voted to use it for the entire three-year under-graduate degree. This gave rise to quite a furore outside the University. I was stupefied to read in *Die Burger* that academics had been 'ordered' to teach in both Afrikaans and English, and once the story was out it ran in that way for quite a while. I invited Senate (which had to ratify the decision) to refer the matter back to the Faculty Board for another vote. That duly happened, and the Faculty Board came up unanimously with the same result. By that time, however, with the 'taaldebat' in full swing, I had realised something: it would be better for me to face the external backlash myself, rather than passing it on to the academics who had actually taken the decision. Taking the blame is part of the job of a Rector, and I was acutely aware of the cultural pressures that could be brought to bear on individual academics from around the 'braaivleis' (barbecue) fires.

On this issue, as with steering Stellenbosch in a new direction, and indeed as with change management generally, the test of leadership of an institution is not only what happens while you are there, but also what happens after you have left. If, as many of the identity-warriors preferred to believe, the changes at Stellenbosch were only due to an idiosyncratic and autocratic Rector, the T-option (for example) would have been cancelled the day I left office. That did not happen. In fact, a decade later it seems that the ship has largely been turned, even though conservative forces continue to make waves and whip up storms. The language policy we instituted in 2002 was still in use long after I had left, and eventually morphed into the kind of pragmatic compromise that I had hoped for from the outset. Upon my departure, Stellenbosch University, through its somewhat tortuous three-stage process, appointed a coloured Afrikaans-speaking theologian as Rector,

Russel Botman, who made the concept of 'hope' the cornerstone of his tenure.[23]

A change of mind can be a painful process, particularly when it is about sharing something you regard as precious, and your own. And yet the Stellenbosch community made great strides in that direction. This became clear to me when I read a statement from one of our students applying for a trip we organised annually to campuses in the USA for upcoming student leaders:

> I am a black proud South African woman that prides herself on being an African, a South African, a Matie![24] ... I look forward to a time when my grandchildren will be Maties and I can say to them that I was one of the leaders of my time that pushed for diversity and multi-culturalism, cultural preservation and equality for all.

On diversity, quality and equality

To round off my two tales, I summarise here in general terms, the conclusions I have reached over the course of my career in various countries regarding the interplay between diversity, quality and equality. Few would deny that a good higher education sector needs a diversity of universities, and all of us would like quality throughout that diversity. So there must be universities that are good, but different, and hence good in different ways. UCT and Stellenbosch are both good, but certainly different, and that is no bad thing. Each can, and should be, good in its own way, while still sharing a common set of academic values.

Mostly, however, our discussion of diversity in higher education is about diversity *within* a university – a diversity of people, very likely, but more importantly a diversity of ideas and talents. I hold the view that diversity has an inherent educational value. For this view, I would offer two reasons. First, learning requires engaging with the unknown. A university is an institute of learning, and we will learn more from those people, those ideas, those phenomena and those circumstances that we do not know, than from those we know only too well. Socio-diversity is valuable to the intellectual environment of a university in somewhat the same way as biodiversity is valuable to the natural environment. (This is one reason why I felt then, as I do now, that Stellenbosch should play a special role in language diversity.) Second, ability can pop up anywhere. You could find a mathematical genius

---

23 Russel Botman died in office on 14 June 2014.
24 Students at Stellenbosch University are called 'Maties'.

in a small town in India, a music legend from working-class Liverpool, a college dropout who becomes a global technology guru, or a world statesman amongst the Xhosas.[25] Therefore, we should cast our net wide, and encourage the rise of ability without preconceived ideas as to where it may be found. Ability raises ability, and learning sparks off learning.

At Stellenbosch, I summarised the view that diversity has an inherent educational value in the phrase *quality needs diversity*.[26] Diversity is not a sufficient condition for quality, but it is necessary, in the sense that, without allowing diversity into our frame of reference, we will not attain true quality.

However, when you do have a diversity of people you also raise a risk, which is the risk of inequality. Where I work now, in the UK, it has been remarked that the English have a genius for turning diversity into hierarchy, and this rather neatly illustrates the risk.[27] When diversity turns into hierarchy, it means that we have turned from an obvious truth about difference of categories to a much less obvious supposition that those categories are not equal. In other words, we turn from an observation of fact to a value judgement. 'Different' is neutral, but 'unequal' is not. The risk, then, is that we will negate the very effects we seek, because the inequality inherent in a presumed hierarchical ordering is prejudicial both against learning from others and against leaving space for the unexpected. If diversity is Dr Jekyll, then hierarchy is Mr Hyde, and the presumption of inequality is what turns the former into the latter. Hierarchy makes a mockery of diversity, and is inimical to the pursuit of quality relative to context.

Inequality is a risk on utilitarian grounds, on social grounds and on moral grounds. It is a risk on utilitarian grounds because it may signal a failure to turn diversity to advantage as a driver of learning and a source of innovation. It is a risk on social grounds because unequal societies demonstrably have a higher incidence of social problems.[28] And it is a risk on moral grounds because it may signal a denial of natural rights or social justice.

---

25 Ramanujan, John Lennon, Steve Jobs and Nelson Mandela.
26 I coined this phrase in the title of a speech at the centenary celebrations of the Rhodes Trust at Stellenbosch University in 2003. The speech appears in full in Botha (2007) *Anatomy of a Transformer*, pp.83–87.
27 Sir Howard Newby, VC of Liverpool University, and previously VC at the University of the West of England and VC at Southampton University.
28 This point has been extensively argued in Wilkinson, R. & Pickett, K. (2009) *The Spirit Level – Why Equality Is Better for Everyone* (Penguin Books: London).

To mitigate the risk of inequality, we may institute a countervailing force, which is an equality agenda. Equality is one of the axioms of a liberal democracy. Thomas Jefferson, with some help from Benjamin Franklin, introduced the American Declaration of Independence with the assertion that all men (sic) are created equal. This is to say that, fundamentally, as a human being, leaving aside all contingent circumstances, each of us is worth as much as any one of us. We are equally endowed with human dignity, we are equal before the law, as citizens we have equal rights and responsibilities, and we all have an equal vote in determining who should exercise governance over those rights and responsibilities.

Arguably, if there were no diversity, there would be no need for an equality agenda. But diversity is real, and so there is a need for equality. The equality agenda has to do with making sure that the axiom of equality is not contravened. Like all axioms, the value of equality is an unprovable assumption rather than a self-evident truth. Nonetheless, it is an assumption strongly and commonly held, because it guarantees natural rights and social justice. Not contravening the axiom of equality means that no individual should be disadvantaged – or, indeed, advantaged – simply by virtue of belonging to any particular group, or displaying any particular group characteristic. In the educational sphere, the equality agenda accepts that not all individuals have equal intellectual ability, just as we do not all have equal physical or artistic or musical ability. It is because we accept that while we are equal as humans we are different as people that we have, over time and with some difficulty, decided to institute measures to ensure that the strong will not exploit the weak, or the many the few, or the able the unable. The equality agenda starts from the premise that natural ability is an individual trait, and that no conclusion regarding the ability of an individual should be drawn only on the basis of their belonging to or identifying with a particular group.[29]

Essentially, therefore, the aim of the equality agenda is to decouple circumstance from destiny. Where you were born, what culture or religion you belong to, how old you are, how rich or poor you or your parents are, what your sexual orientation is, whether or not you have any disability – no such manifestation of diversity should deny you any educational opportunity, nor impede your levels of attainment. Ability should be able to access opportunity regardless of circumstance.

---

29 I should emphasise that, by 'group', I mean a social group, not just an artificially defined collection of people. Otherwise, it would not be difficult to construct counter-examples.

I would not say that I had all this figured out in exactly these terms when I started a Numeracy Centre, or expounded the principle that quality needs diversity. Both at UCT and at Stellenbosch, values and conviction played as much a part in what I did as logic or calculation. But I do think that conviction has stood the test of reasoning, and reasoning has stood the test of value. The interplay between reasoning and values illustrates what I regard as the two fundamental questions about our academic work, and about the nature of a university. The first, which is a matter of quality, is to ask what we are good at. The second, which is a matter of equality – or, more broadly, our role in civil society – is to ask what we are good *for*. I would recommend both these questions to any academic, and to any university.

chapter 6

Academic leadership during institutional restructuring

Rolf Stumpf

In 2002, Rolf Stumpf was appointed Vice-Chancellor and Principal (VCP) of the University of Port Elizabeth, which was earmarked to merge with the Port Elizabeth Technikon and the local campus of Vista University in Port Elizabeth to form the Nelson Mandela Metropolitan University (NMMU). He was Vice-Chancellor (VC) of NMMU until 2007. The story of the complex merger and its leadership is the subject of Stumpf's chapter.

Stumpf spent his childhood in KwaZulu-Natal, having been born into a German-speaking family who instilled in him a lifelong appreciation for the value of education, a love for books and literature, and an abiding love for music.

He attended the University of Pretoria on a full scholarship, where he studied Mathematics and other science-related subjects, and, out of curiosity, also enrolled for English. He switched over to English, Economics and History while retaining Mathematics, and also choosing Statistics for timetable reasons. Paradoxically, he ended up doing his PhD in Statistics, which caused him to have great sympathy with students who 'don't know what they wish to study'.

At the end of his third year, he accepted a lectureship in the Department of Statistics at the University of Pretoria, which he greatly enjoyed. Although he had attended an Afrikaans-speaking university, Stumpf retained an abiding interest in English, bringing his children up as English-speakers.

He also decided early on to adopt a scientifically informed point of view in pursuing the well-being of society, remaining politically independent as far as possible.

His next job was helping to develop financing models for education in the then Department of National Education. This took him beyond the confines of the financing of education into issues of governance, broad education-system policy, programme and curriculum design, student access and development, education information systems, stakeholder engagement, and so on. He was appointed Deputy Director-General of National Education in the late 1980s. This was followed by a stint as President of the Human Sciences Research Council (HSRC) from 1993 to 1998.

W hat is remarkable about the period in which I was in the national department (1984–1993) is the role played by some universities, under the leadership of their vice-chancellors (VCs) and principals, in the eventual demise of apartheid and the apartheid-based higher education system. This chapter does not attempt to encompass the vital role of higher education leadership in leading universities as instruments of social change in the interest of justice, freedom and democracy for all in South Africa, but instead addresses the somewhat more circumscribed topic of leadership during times of radical institutional change and restructuring.

The period 1994 to 2004 marked a period of sustained higher education system development, policy development, and institutional renewal. This was to be expected given the demise of the previous apartheid-based higher education system. This period started with the report of the National Commission on Higher Education (NCHE) in 1996, followed by: the *White Paper on Higher Education Transformation* in 1997; the promulgation of the Higher Education Act, Act 101 of 1997; the establishment of the Council on Higher Education (CHE) and its Higher Education Quality Committee in 1998; the introduction of a new higher education management information system in 1999; the proposals for a drastic restructuring of the higher education system by the CHE, commonly referred to as the 'Size and Shape Report', in 2000; the publishing of the *National Plan for Higher Education* in 2001; and, in 2002, proposals by a ministerial working group on a range of institutional mergers and institutional incorporations. This was followed by a formal, government-approved plan for restructuring the higher education institutional landscape later in 2002. From 2003 to 2004, three further significant policy initiatives were launched, namely: obligatory enrolment planning by higher education institutions; the introduction of an approval system for the mix of programmes and qualifications to be offered by each university; and a new funding model replacing the previous South African Post-Secondary Education (SAPSE) system.

In many ways, universities were struggling to keep up with all these developments (which at the best of times would have stretched the capacity and ability of most institutions beyond measure) when government announced its plan to reconfigure the higher education institutional landscape. This plan eventuated in the establishment of a higher education institutional landscape consisting of: six comprehensive universities (merging universities with technikons and/or expanding the mandates of traditional universities to include technikon programmes); six universities of technology (all being former technikons); 11 general universities; and two national institutes for higher education.

As part of this plan, the University of Port Elizabeth (UPE) was to incorporate the local campus of Vista University, and, after that, merge with the Port Elizabeth Technikon (PET) to form the new Nelson Mandela Metropolitan University (NMMU). In my roles as Vice-Chancellor and Principal (VCP) of UPE from 2002, as Interim VCP of the newly formed NMMU in 2004, and as substantive VCP of NMMU from 2005, my main tasks were: first, to steer UPE into the merger during the pre-merger phase; second, to initiate the steps for creating NMMU in the interim merger phases; and, then, in the immediate post-merger phase, to establish NMMU as a well-functioning comprehensive university embodying high academic standards.

In this chapter, I concentrate on the leadership and management challenges in times of radical institutional restructuring, illustrating with examples from my NMMU experience. This is based on the assumption that, while in other cases of institutional restructuring the contexts may differ, the basic challenges faced in redefining an institution strategically, structurally, and operationally would largely be similar. Furthermore, although the context I address is one of incisive institutional restructuring involving multiple institutions, many of the challenges would also be applicable to restructuring within a university, for example, of academic faculties or departments or of support sections. In fact, much of what is covered would be applicable to leading and managing a higher education institution in more stable and more 'normal' circumstances.

Leadership and management

Before addressing the various challenges likely to be encountered in institutional restructuring exercises, I touch on some issues regarding leadership and management. These issues are raised in the context of general leadership and management requirements during times of institutional restructuring as I encountered them, and are not meant to represent a scholarly description of the differences between these two concepts.

In institutional restructuring, a clear understanding of the differences and relationship between leadership and management is particularly important. The pressures accompanying institutional restructuring can easily lead to them being unduly conflated, which, in turn, can lead institutional heads to become sidetracked, or to become overly involved with management and operational issues at the cost of neglecting direction-setting and strategic issues. In fact, one of the great challenges for institutional heads in institutional restructuring is to strike an appropriate balance between leadership and management. This balance is likely to be influenced quite strongly by institutional contexts and may even be influenced by the kind of person the institutional head is.

I have found that some of the most vital *leadership requirements* within the context of institutional restructuring, which by no means represent an exhaustive list, are as follows:

- Setting a compelling institutional vision and mission as part of the strategic direction of the reconfigured institution that the majority of the academic and non-academic staff and the students can support. For higher education institutions, this should always involve a primary emphasis on a university's three core functions of teaching and learning, research, and community engagement. It is absolutely vital that leadership of a university is always circumscribed by its nature as an academic institution rather than as a manufacturing concern or a civil-service agency;

- Leading in the setting of a moral and ethical values framework for desired institutional as well as individual behaviour with respect to work responsibilities, internal institutional relations, and external institutional relations. This framework, if not exemplified by the life and behaviour of the head of the university, will simply be meaningless and, in fact, can become counterproductive. One of the major components of this framework has to be the uncompromising pursuit of excellence academically, professionally, and in all other spheres of institutional endeavour;

- Remaining steadfastly on course with the end goals of the restructuring process in view and refusing to be sidetracked from agreed-upon goals and objectives. This is particularly the case in radical institutional restructuring where many unexpected events and even crises may crop up and direct attention away from the main focus. Having said that, it is vitally important that such crises are dealt with forthrightly and that those institutional leaders remain unruffled in all circumstances. This, of course, means that institutional leaders must be able to manage their own stress and tension levels successfully; and

- Consistently separating the issue at hand from the person(s) involved. This is one of the most crucial aspects involved in university leadership, and especially so in the case of institutional restructuring. Universities are institutions dedicated to the free and unfettered expression of views and opinions concerning the way they pursue their primary academic and supporting activities. University heads will, inevitably, be criticised and even be vehemently opposed by some who feel that the institution would be better served by another approach on a particular issue. This means institutional leaders must be able to listen to, and hear, what others are putting forward as part of an objective evaluation of what would be the best course in the interest of the institution. Universities abound where VCPs, unable to separate the person and the issue, have made mortal enemies of some staff members to the detriment of the institution as a whole.

Next, I discuss some of the most vital *management requirements* within the context of institutional restructuring. Once again, what follows is by no means intended to represent an exhaustive list of issues, but are the ones I found most critical:

- Finding an appropriate mix between executive management (sometimes referred to as 'managerialism') and collegial management, particularly in university restructuring, is vital. Not doing so could either reduce the restructuring to a purely technical and mechanical process, void of any people considerations, or enmesh the restructuring process in excruciatingly slow, and sometimes severely compromised, decision-making processes characterised by taking soft or popular decisions.

  Many universities in South Africa have incorporated some aspects of executive management into their management processes. They have done so in order to cope with the newer type of institutional management challenges which require decisive, quicker decision-making. In doing so, they have generally, however, not entirely abandoned more traditional forms of collegial management, which is still very much the favoured management model among academic staff. In virtually all universities in South Africa, this model in which the academic manager is merely the 'first amongst equals' still largely characterises academic faculties and departments.

Especially in times of radical institutional restructuring, it is necessary that the institutional leadership, and, in particular, the VCP, has a thorough understanding of when to apply which management approach, and how these are interrelated. It is, furthermore, important for institutional leadership to realise that some issues may require a collegial approach at the beginning, then move towards a greater emphasis on executive management decision-making, and possibly end up with a collegial management emphasis in the final phase again, or the other way round. In this regard, it is vital that institutional leadership is able to be flexible in identifying which issues are best dealt with at their various stages, and through which management approach. For example, a new resource-allocation model for a restructured institution would typically start off strongly within the executive management mode, then after that probably move to a more collegially dominated assessment phase, and finally back to an executive management mode for finalisation. I found that this type of managerial flexibility was particularly important when developing an academic plan for the new institution, for new academic structures, and for new academic staffing structures, to name but a few;

- Developing sound and feasible implementation plans to give effect to agreed institutional strategic and direction-setting initiatives and goals. These plans should demonstrate an effective and efficient utilisation of the large variety of institutional resources in pursuing agreed strategic goals and objectives of the institution. These resources can take the form of human capacity, financial capacity, infrastructural resources, etc.;

- Establishing institutional sustainability in a broader sense through the development of a range of institutional plans, systems, policies and processes that promote good governance and sound management, and stimulate institutional endeavour in achieving the agreed-upon vision and mission. These measures should act as a safeguard for the institution and individuals in the institution, including the institutional head, against irrational and capricious acts, and advance the equal and equitable treatment of all staff and students;

- Developing an organisational structure based on a set of institutionally acceptable principles and points of departure. Universities in the past have been notorious for allowing structures to develop around a particular person, often resulting in extremely ineffective institutional organisational structures, which then have to be dismantled at considerable cost once the person concerned has left the employ of the university. In particular, VCPs should avoid enlarging their own office staff beyond absolutely necessary levels;

- Setting up a system and developing policies clearly demarcating areas and levels of responsibility and accountability for all staff members, students and institutional structures. Every staff member and institutional structure should be absolutely clear on the boundaries of their duties and responsibilities. I found that a particular challenge of managing a university, especially during times of institutional restructuring, resided in bridging the traditional gap between academe and administration, and establishing a cohesive institutional work and delivery environment.

Against this background, one of the first issues to be resolved during the period of institutional restructuring is likely to be that of how rigid a distinction should be maintained between leadership and management at the level of the institution's head. In the case of the NMMU merger, both in the pre-merger phase and in the immediate post-merger phase, after consultation with the Council, it was decided that the VCP – in other words, me – should be the face of the merger.

Practically, this meant that overseeing the merger in its entirety was my responsibility and that I should not devolve the management of the merger to, say, one of the Deputy Vice-Chancellors (DVCs). To support me, a high-level merger project office was established by seconding one or two academic staff members and one or two non-academic staff members to my office. It was vital to ensure a 'mean and lean' merger project office in order to enable the institution to still carry out all its daily operational responsibilities while at the same time planning for, and proceeding with, the merger.

While it would generally be impossible to drive through a radical institutional restructuring such as was the case for NMMU without such a support structure, one of the enduring challenges was to avoid any perception that the project team, even in practice, constituted a privileged inner circle and would be able to usurp the traditional roles of university structures such as executive management, Senate, faculty boards, and so on.

In our case, we achieved this by not according any undue status to the merger project office by including some of its members in the executive management and Senate for the duration of the merger to avoid parallel decision-making structures. A further measure that proved useful was having more frequent meetings of Council and Council committees, executive management, and Senate and its executive committee during the pre-merger and immediate post-merger phase. Taking all things into consideration, while we could undeniably have done better, this approach worked reasonably well for NMMU, and undue tensions between the merger project office and the remainder of the institution were largely absent. A year or so into the post-merger period, the merger project office was formally dismantled having done what it had set out to do.

Post-merger position and remuneration of the Vice-Chancellor

Before discussing some more specific leadership and management challenges likely to be encountered during a period of institutional restructuring based on the NMMU experience, two issues need to be covered, namely: the desirability of whether the driver of radical institutional change should remain at the helm of the university after completion of the main merger and incorporation initiatives; and when a decision on the remuneration level of the first-appointed staff member of the new institution, being the VC, should be made. Introducing these two matters may seem surprising, but, within them, important leadership and management principles are at stake.

Views on both these questions are likely to vary considerably. The longer-term position of the pre-merger and immediate post-merger VC will, in part, depend on the speed with which such a restructuring has been carried out. Most business and human resources manage-ment experts will argue, 'the quicker the better'. In NMMU's case, agreement was reached between me and the Council that the main features of the new university would be in place within three years. Furthermore, although the Council offered me the standard five-year contract, this was reduced to three years at my request. This request was based on the view of business and management experts that the person driving the implementation of the merger, assuming that it was done properly, should make way as soon as possible after the merger for someone who could come into the position without carry-ing any undue merger baggage. Whatever the view, the crucial point is that, at the outset, clarity on this question should be established between the institutional head and the council of the university.

In hindsight, in our case, this decision, which was known in the insti-tution, had both advantages and disadvantages. It certainly provided an impetus for me to do as much as possible during the three-year appointment period in order to hand over a fully functioning merged institution to a new VC. It also conveyed a clear signal to the institution that this merger, with its accompanying uncertainties and anxieties, was not going to last forever, and that a clear end-date had been set for it. In addition, it sent a strong signal that I was not arranging a cushy post-merger job guarantee for myself while other staff members had to wait and see what their prospects in the new institution were going to be. However, it turned out that three years were a little too short a period and that a further six to 12 months would have better served to tie up all the merger issues satisfactorily.

The second question, concerning when a decision of the VC's remuneration should be taken, may at first glance seem trite and not worthy of attention. However, it masks a crucial leadership principle, that the head of the institution cannot expect the staff to adopt a specific ruling but exempt himself or herself from that ruling unless there are sound reasons for doing so.

In the case of the NMMU, this ruling refers to a decision taken that, in the interim phase of the merger, no remuneration adjustments would be made to any staff member's remuneration until all staff had been placed into new staffing positions in a new organisational structure. Such remuneration adjustments would be subject to a new and harmonised NMMU remuneration policy as approved by Council. The background to this decision was that it quickly became apparent that average remuneration levels at UPE were the lowest, followed by those of the PET, and finally those of Vista University's campus in Port Elizabeth (PE), which were the highest. Harmonisation to the highest remuneration levels was out of the question, and the above decision was taken in terms of ensuring fairness and consistency for all staff members.

Applying this principle consistently would have meant that my remuneration, although I was the first substantively appointed staff member of the NMMU, should also await the finalisation of a comprehensive new remuneration policy for the new institution, and, in the intervening period, be remunerated at my previous level. This decision proved invaluable in withstanding countless efforts by staff members to obtain a special salary dispensation for themselves prior to the finalisation of all appointments to NMMU, and keeping the new institution's remuneration costs in check.

Specific leadership and management challenges

Next, I discuss a selected number of specific leadership and management challenges in times of institutional restructuring. The issues covered do not claim to represent a complete list of such issues, and neither are they arranged in any specific order of importance. They have been chosen to highlight different challenges, such as: those of a more strategic nature; those which are more people- and communication-oriented; those which are related to organisational structures; those of a strongly technical nature; and those related to institutional relationships, particularly between senior management and the council.

Opposition to institutional restructuring

It would be surprising indeed if institutional restructuring did not elicit some form of opposition. The more radical and extensive the restructuring, the more intense the opposition in some quarters is likely to be. In a university, probably more so than in any other type of institution, opposition to such restructuring should not be ignored or downplayed in any way. It should be faced head-on; the institutional leadership should engage in discussion and debate, sometimes over a protracted period, with those who oppose the intended restructuring.

Opposition to institutional restructuring can spring from genuine concerns that the restructuring will weaken the academic standing, and particularly the research endeavours, of a participating institution that prides itself on its record in this regard. It can also stem from strongly held, often stereotyped, views of others involved in the institutional restructuring as somehow being 'lower' in the academic pecking order than they are, and from fears in respect of job security and career prospects. In addition, of course, there are always some who would oppose any form of institutional restructuring as they would any form of change.

In managing such opposition, it is vital that the institutional head is able to present a convincing argument of the academic, organisational, administrative, financial, and infrastructural benefits of the proposed restructuring, with an emphasis first and foremost on the academic benefits. This argument should include the likely benefits to the broader community as well as to business and civil society. The case for institutional restructuring should not gloss over any potential negatives to the envisaged restructuring, but face them fairly and squarely. This case should form the basis for a wide range of consultative discussions with various groupings of staff and students, including specific structures such as executive management, senate, faculty boards, students' representative bodies, alumni association or convocation, and so on. The final documentation setting out the case for the proposed institutional restructuring should reflect the inputs from these various discussions and also give an indication, even if a very broad one, of how the likely challenges are to be managed.

Obviously, obtaining unanimous support for a proposed restructuring, while desirable, is highly unlikely. Before submitting the final case for restructuring to a university's council, it is prudent to represent the case to the university community. In UPE's case, this was done by calling a university assembly rather than dealing with each of the university structures and groupings individually again. Thereafter, a final set of arguments was presented to Council for a final decision.

This approach has advantages and disadvantages. In UPE's case, some members of Senate felt that the proposed merger with the two institutions with weaker research records would undermine UPE's research track record, which had been built up over many years. They were of the opinion that Senate's view on the envisaged merger should have played a stronger, and even decisive, role in comparison with the views of other institutional structures and groupings. In fact, at the height of the merger, some former UPE professors argued that UPE should have challenged government's merger decision in court, despite the fact that this viewpoint had been aired in the original discussions debating the 'pros' and 'cons' of the merger, and roundly discarded as counterproductive. In any event, it is interesting that these fears concerning threats to the research endeavours and outputs never materialised, and that NMMU during the post-merger period has made very significant progress in improving its research endeavours and outputs.

Establishing mutual institutional and personal trust relationships

Despite efforts to portray mergers and some other forms of institutional restructuring, such as institutional incorporations, as involving 'equal' parties, this is in reality seldom the case. Perceptions usually abound of so-called 'senior' and 'junior' partners in such an exercise, with the junior partners fearing and resisting any hint of domination by the senior partners. Furthermore, strongly held stereotypes of one another usually contribute to establishing high initial levels of distrust and suspicion of motives between parties involved in institutional restructuring. These levels of distrust and suspicion normally characterise the pre-merger and immediate post-merger phase, and can become extremely debilitating if not addressed frankly and forthrightly.

In NMMU's case, this was no different. Vista University's campus in PE was extremely distrustful of both UPE and PET's abilities to grasp and take on board the fact that, according to them, they served an entirely different type of student. Interestingly, once they had been incorporated into the then UPE in 2004, the converse was actually found to be true, with UPE far better equipped to support students from academically and financially disadvantaged communities.

UPE staff members, for their part, generally felt that the applied and career preparatory teaching, learning and research focus of PET inevitably translated into inferior academic standards and academic outputs, and that little if any academic commonality existed between the two institutions. PET staff, on the other hand, seemed to feel that UPE was too arrogant and was not measuring up in terms of the required levels of responsiveness and relevance of its academic and research programmes. In addition, they felt that they had established far more constructive relationships with the broader PE communities, especially business and industry. An important way of changing such levels of distrust and suspicion is in composing restructuring task teams in such a manner that, as far as possible, 'equal' representation of the restructuring parties is seen to occur. The question of convenors of such task teams could be resolved by arranging for co-convenors from the parties involved. Eliminating such distrust on the academic level as quickly as possible was in our case vital. One way of approaching this was to select a teaching and learning programme which seemed, on the face of it, fairly similar in the participating institutions. The selected academic programme was then subjected to scrutiny by academic staff from all the parties involved with a view to identifying commonalities and differences. The interactions emerging from such an exercise contributed significantly to breaking down mistrust and suspicion. In the case of NMMU, this approach quickly showed that, in some instances, two distinct academic programmes would have to be maintained, while, in other cases, a single academic programme providing for 'streams' in the later years of study seemed feasible. A similar approach could be followed in respect of selecting an appropriate research programme for closer analysis.

Normally, institutional restructuring involving higher education institutions will present three distinct phases: these are the pre-, the interim, and the immediate post-restructuring phases. It is vital that, in all these phases, the issue of establishing acceptable levels of trust is addressed by the relevant institutional or divisional heads. This would be the task of the interim head(s) in the interim phase, and of the substantive head(s) in the immediate post-merger phase. Without first establishing acceptable trust levels within the emerging new institution, institutional leadership will find it has to deal with subtle acts of 'sabotage' and unnecessary 'point-scoring' by staff members in the various restructuring phases.

A number of institutional and functional areas present themselves for establishing acceptable levels of trust. One area involves the composition of interim structures, such as executive management, senate, and so on. Another entails widespread and regular communication between the institutional leadership and rank-and-file staff members and students on 'on the ground' restructuring issues. Finally, another area involves the vexing issue of allocation of physical space to staff members in the new institution's building infrastructure.

In NMMU's case, I first constituted an interim executive committee that reflected the highest possible degree of equal representation between participating institutions. This surprised many, including, to some extent, the interim Council, which had expected the opportunity to be used to cement UPE's dominance in the further unfolding of the restructuring process. In fact, some members of UPE's Senate felt that this was an opportunity lost. On the more positive side, it allayed fears in PET and Vista campus quarters that they were now in for being 'UPE-tised'.

Second, I made it my business to interact with at least one institutional grouping every day. Initially, these interactions were arranged per institution, but, as soon as possible, they progressed to interactions involving groupings across the institutions such as library staff, or information technology staff, or similar academic departments. These interactions, which popularly became known as 'tea and scones' sessions, were aimed at capturing vexing, on-the-ground restructuring challenges from individual staff members and students. After every five or so of these sessions, the issues raised would be arranged in categories and presented to the interim executive management for discussion and feedback at the next tea and scones session. In addition, the issues as well as the proposed ways of resolving them were communicated regularly to the entire staff and student community in the form of 'merger communiques' from my office. This approach assisted enormously in assuring staff members that their on-the-ground issues were not only being heard, but were also receiving executive management's attention. Furthermore, this also ensured that the institutional leadership remained in touch with people's issues, thus avoiding the danger of the entire restructuring process simply becoming a technically driven exercise.

Third, during the immediate post-restructuring phase, a 'placement committee' recommended physical offices for staff members in the new organisational structure of NMMU across the various campuses which now constituted the new university. One of these recommendations was that my office, which at that stage was situated at the former UPE's main campus, should move to the main campus of the former PET. Symbolically, the fact that the former UPE VC was willing, as NMMU VC, to move his office to the campus of the former PET served as a powerful signal that the days of inter-institutional rivalry and competition were over, and had been replaced by a common NMMU ethos.

Development of a new organisational and staffing structure

The development of a new organisational and staffing structure represents one of the most daunting challenges to be faced in institutional restructuring. In order to negate the debilitating effects of job insecurity on job performance, this should usually be commenced before most of the strategies, institutional plans, and staffing policies are fully in place. Furthermore, the actual cost of institutional restructuring will vary as the restructuring progresses and as new and unexpected costs emerge, making it very difficult to assess how many staff positions may need to be scrapped, and how many new ones should be established, before finalisation of the restructuring process.

An institutionally accepted strategic plan for the new institution will, in all likelihood, not yet have been developed at the stage when the above issue has to be addressed. This is because it is very difficult to get staff members, especially academic staff members, to work together constructively on the shape and size, academic direction, and emphasis of a new institution if they do not know whether they will be part of it or not. What should, however, be available will be the broad strategic direction which the new institution will follow. In addition, the strategic plans of the existing institutions involved in the restructuring should also be available for use. The same goes for academic plans, if available.

Although developing the organisational structure of the new institution in its entirety as soon as possible is crucial, it is even more urgent to start with the development of a new academic organisational structure, and an academic staffing structure. This follows since it is important that the academic staff members are enabled to continue their 'normal' academic duties and pursuits in the full knowledge of their role in the new institution or entity, in order not to adversely affect the institution's academic endeavours and outputs. In this regard, senate and/or the senate executive committee, should be involved in the task teams exploring the various possibilities.

The development of a new academic structure is particularly prone to prolonged battles due to personal and vested academic interests, and should be shielded from undue dominance by prominent academic figures on campus. In order to avoid academic structures being built around individuals, it should be based on a number of points of departure on which senate should reach agreement before they are applied. Some of these points of departure also need a considerable amount of discussion before being finalised and before they can serve as useful instruments in the development of an academic structure.

We found the following points of departure particularly important:

- The proposed broad strategic thrust of the new institution interpreted from an academic perspective;
- Existing knowledge areas covered by the various institutional programme and qualifications mix (PQM) profiles and the knowledge areas to be covered in the new institution;
- Existing academic strengths and weaknesses in the entities involved in the restructuring;
- National, regional and local socio-economic development needs interpreted from a knowledge perspective;
- Criteria and requirements of accreditation agencies (if applicable);
- Advantages and disadvantages of a three-tier academic structure consisting of faculties, schools, and departments, compared with a two-tier academic structure consisting of faculties and departments;
- Accommodating disciplinary, multidisciplinary and inter-disciplinary knowledge emphases;
- Customs and practices in establishing academic structures in other institutions nationally and internationally; and
- Sustainability criteria in terms of minimum full-time equivalent (FTE) student numbers and appropriately qualified FTE staff numbers for faculties, schools (if adopted) and departments.[1]

Obviously, points of departure such as these should not be applied rigidly. It is always possible that, for very specific reasons, a particular knowledge area which does not satisfy all the criteria, is still deemed fit to include.

In NMMU's case, a step-wise process was followed in first finalising the points of departure; thereafter reaching agreement on the basic set of faculties to be accommodated within the new institution; and thereafter reaching agreement on the within-faculty structures in terms of schools and departments. In this process, some faculties opted for a three-tier and some for a two-tier structure where their size and other

---

1   The ratio of the total number of paid hours during a period (part-time, full-time, contracted) to the number of working hours in that period, Mondays through Fridays. The ratio units are FTE units or equivalent employees working full-time. In other words, one FTE is equivalent to one employee working full-time; from http://www.businessdictionary.com/definition/full-time-equivalent-FTE.html#ixzz3hMWdH8nd. Accessed 7 August 2015.

factors did not support the establishment of schools in addition to departments. We found it was important not to insist on a 'one-size-fits-all' approach, due to the great variation in size of faculties, with Management and Business Science, for example, having in excess of 5000 FTE students and Law having a much smaller cohort of around 1 500 FTE students. By and large, this process worked reasonably well, although it had its hiccups and periods where emotion threatened to overrule rationality. It helped that I personally participated in most of the development processes of the new academic structure, particularly where deadlocks and stalemates required some or other definite resolution.

However, despite this, one or two developments which should probably not have been accepted were in the end accepted simply for the sake of making progress. In hindsight, this should not have been done, as it is usually very difficult to later undo that which should have been done correctly from the beginning.

The next step involving the development of staffing structures for the various academic units is, if anything, likely to prove even more difficult, and is normally characterised by deep emotion as academic staff members face the intensely personal issue of whether they have a role in the new institution or not. This is compounded where collegial management in academic faculties has been so firmly entrenched that any form of executive management by deans and departmental heads is fiercely resisted.

Once again, it is vital that a set of criteria be developed that can guide decision-making in this regard. Even so, the difficulty is likely to be that existing staffing structures exhibit many historical anomalies when assessed against a rational set of criteria. Despite all efforts to set aside existing staffing structures and to 'think out of the box', this could prove to be too much to ask of many academic staff members whose futures are at stake.

The development of such a set of criteria should, if done properly, be the subject of considerable analysis and investigation. In this regard, staff allocation systems of other universities can be very helpful and should be examined with a view to developing a staff allocation system for a restructured institution. Factors that typically play a role in staff allocation formulas would be: senior lecturer equivalents (SLEs) based on a weighted relationship between the posts of senior professor (if applicable), professor, associate professor, senior lecturer, lecturer, and junior lecturer; FTE student to FTE academic staff ratios for different knowledge areas and for undergraduate and postgraduate studies; faculty FTE undergraduate and postgraduate enrolments;

student graduation numbers and rates; research outputs (publications, research masters and doctoral graduations); government subsidy income per faculty member; and anticipated tuition fee income per faculty member, to list a few.

In NMMU's case, once interim deans of faculties had been appointed, they were asked to initiate processes (for which extensive guidelines were developed) for proposing an academic staffing structure for each faculty, its schools (if applicable) and its academic departments. One of these was that the proposals should not be built around people or existing structures, although both these aspects would be taken into account in a final staff placement exercise; another was some indication of cost limits to be applied. Faculties were also asked to make proposals on within-faculty administrative support, and, in cases where needed, for technical laboratory support.

Most interim deans found this an extremely frustrating and difficult exercise; in general, the proposals they received were completely unrealistic in terms of affordability. Many academic staff members and heads of departments saw this merely as an opportunity to obtain long-wished-for academic posts, which they felt their departments were entitled to. In some cases, clear evidence of 'empire-building' emerged. In addition, interim deans, due to their 'interim' status, often felt powerless to intervene and bring the proposals back down to earth, so to speak.

By agreement with Senate, these proposals were first vetted by the merger project office for clarity and any errors, without any form of assessment taking place. Thereafter, I led a smaller task team that met a small delegation from each faculty who presented their proposals. This task team also included the interim DVCs, interim heads of Human Resources and of Finance, staff from the Institutional Planning Office, and an interim dean or two from faculties other than the one presenting its staffing proposals. At times, these sessions were quite difficult, particularly so for the interim deans. They felt themselves pressed between a 'rock and a hard place': their colleagues in the faculty expected them to 'fight management' and achieve what had been proposed, but they knew that the proposals were unaffordable and could not realistically be defended in the broader institutional context.

In addition, this phase of the institutional restructuring demon-strated the need for greater synchronisation between the many restructuring initiatives that were pursued simultaneously. It might seem ideal to set out the various merger initiatives in a sequential arrangement of one initiative following after the other. The fact that institutional restructuring is best approached over the shortest possible time span makes this impossible, and this means that some issues are inevitably going to be initiated while others, which should have been concluded first as a prerequisite, are still being finalised. In institutional restructuring exercises, there will be many instances in which there is simply no way round such dilemmas.

As an example, I consider the case of developing NMMU's academic and non-academic staffing structure. When we began, only one substantive appointment had been made, namely mine as VC. Try as we might to not develop staffing structures with people in mind, this proved impossible in the face of the desperate need of staff members to ensure a future in the new institution. It also meant that interim managers, on the whole, were somewhat reluctant to take hard and unpopular decisions for fear of jeopardising their own institutional futures. Ideally, staff should perhaps all first have been assured of placement to 'free' them up to participate more objectively in the development of a staffing structure. Practically, this was just not possible, as the staffing structure of the new institution would determine the role that instruments such as accelerated natural attrition, voluntary severance and, ultimately, retrenchment, would play in the new institution. In addition, Council somewhat unrealistically, as it would turn out later, expected large staff cuts owing to the supposedly widespread 'duplication' of functions and posts which was expected to emerge during the restructuring.

In NMMU's case, and particularly in the case of developing a new staffing structure, it meant that I was the one who had to ask the uncomfortable questions of managers regarding their proposed faculty or section structures, and the accompanying proposed staffing structures, and who mostly had to take the hard decision of saying 'no' to clearly indefensible proposals.

This particular experience served to underline for me the reality that, if done quickly and properly, the institutional leader overseeing the brunt of the institutional restructuring, could find it difficult to carry on leading and managing the institution once the institutional restructuring had been completed. In this sense, institutional restructuring could mean that someone should be willing to 'get the job done', and then 'clear out'.

Staff placement and revised conditions of employment

As with the previous issue, the harmonising of different sets of conditions of employment and the actual appointment of existing staff to positions in a new staffing structure are likely to prove extremely contentious and even acrimonious in any type of institutional restructuring.

For many staff members participating in institutional restructuring, this is actually where the 'rubber hits the road'. From a managerial perspective, this aspect is easily the most difficult and stressful part of any institutional restructuring.

The South African Labour Relations Act, Act 66 of 1995 prescribes the framework within which restructuring affecting the employment status of staff members has to be conducted. Since this part of institutional restructuring is most likely to give rise to litigation in some form or other, it is prudent for any institutional head driving a restructuring programme to obtain the services of top labour law specialists for the duration of the restructuring.

On the one hand, this part of the restructuring process is the most emotive from an individual point of view; on the other hand, it is also the most technical, requiring management and recognised unions to work in tandem in ensuring a fair staff placement process. An important step is the development of a new and harmonised set of conditions of employment. This should normally be done as soon as possible and should be formally signed off by all the unions recognised in the participating institutions. It should go hand in hand with the development of a new institutional labour relations framework establishing new bargaining structures, and new union recognition criteria.

In developing such new conditions of employment, a number of matters must be resolved simultaneously, such as the following: To whom will the new conditions of employment apply? If to all appointments in terms of the new staffing structure in the new institution, will remuneration levels be affected or not? And, what happens to leave, medical aid, and retirement benefits accrued in the existing institutions? Answers to these questions depend to a large extent on whether a totally new institution is being created, or simply one consisting of an amalgamation of the existing ones.

In NMMU's case, the development of a new and harmonised set of conditions of employment was one of the very first steps initiated in the interim restructuring period. This resulted in varied reactions from staff members. Some expressed their genuine appreciation for the speedy resolution of such a potentially contentious matter; others merely wished to know if, in addition to the new conditions of employment, the existing ones would be maintained, and, if so, for how long; others yet were mainly concerned with how differences in remuneration levels between existing conditions of employment and the new ones would be resolved; while some were downright angry, and opposed the new conditions of employment vociferously.

Those opposed to the new conditions of employment based their opposition, somewhat surprisingly, on some quite non-fundamental matters, such as annual leave, which was set at a lower level than the then-current leave allocation for staff at PET and at the Vista University campus, but matched by the introduction of research leave, which did not then exist on those campuses; the capping of accrued leave in line with then-current practice at UPE; the harmonisation of parking fees (one staff member wrote to me complaining bitterly that, from one day to the next, he would have to pay double for the same parking spot); managing core office presence within a system of flexitime; and, most surprising of all, the withdrawal of subsidised tea and coffee sessions for staff members from the then-PET where this was accepted practice.

These were some of the issues that were raised by staff members in the tea and scones sessions mentioned earlier. They were also picked up through other communication channels, exposing the depth of the differences in institutional ethos and culture among the participating institutions. This was especially true concerning the role and place of research, as demonstrated by the emotion shown by some regarding the reduction of annual vacation leave in favour of research leave.

However, the existence of a clear process to harmonise the remuneration levels, as expeditiously as possible, in terms of the new conditions of employment of those who had either been 'underpaid' or 'overpaid' (whereby there would not be an absolute reduction of remuneration but rather a gradual easing into the lower remuneration level over a period of up to five years), did much to allay fears and establish confidence in the fairness of treatment amongst staff members.

The next step involved the development of job descriptions for all staffing positions in the new organisational structure, and the subsequent grading of all positions in terms of job complexity. This can be an extremely time-consuming exercise, but extensive guidelines should be developed for assisting all interim managers in drawing up appropriate job descriptions for positions in the new staff structure and thus limiting the time taken up by this exercise.

As job grading invariably is challenged by those expecting a higher job grading for a position similar to the one they were in, or one that they were anticipating to be appointed to, it is prudent, despite the costs involved, to outsource this exercise to agencies specialising in this particular field. It is also vital to have in place a system for dealing with challenges to the outcomes of the job grading process and limiting the number of reviews approved.

Once this exercise has been completed, a remuneration model for the new institution should be developed. As in all cases, this is an extremely technical exercise and involves benchmarking the new institution's remuneration levels with those of similar or competing institutions. It is, thus, advisable to obtain the services of agencies specialising in the development of remuneration models for this step.

The final step comprises either matching existing employees to posts in the new structure, or requiring every existing employee to apply for posts for which they think they meet the requirements. It would be prudent, once again in consultation with the recognised unions, to adopt an approach involving both of these. For example, if an existing employee can demonstrate an overlap of say more than 80 per cent between his/her existing job description and the one for the new post, and if such a post existed in only one of the participating institutions, he/she could simply be matched to the new position. However, if the post in question existed earlier in more than one of the participating institutions, and two or more staff members could thus claim the 'right' to the job, a formal application and appointment process may have to be followed.

Obviously, brand-new positions in the new staffing structure would have to be advertised in the normal way. However, it is usual to give preference to the placement of internal candidates; and only if no suitable candidate comes forward, to then move towards advertising the post externally.

A further management decision to be taken is whether the assigning or appointing of existing staff should occur from top to bottom, or from bottom to top. Opinions on this vary, but, in order not to extend the duration of this process unnecessarily, a 'big bang' approach in tackling as many positions as possible simultaneously may well be best. In the case of NMMU, the latter approach was followed, although where possible, managerial posts were appointed first so that substantively appointed managers could drive the appointment processes further in their sections.

Finally, a system providing for voluntary severance packages and, if necessary, retrenchment procedures should be put in place. The difficulty sometimes encountered with voluntary severance packages is that the people whose services one would ideally like to retain often apply for this option. Conversely, those whose services are more dispensable do not tend to apply. In order to avoid losing high-quality staff, it is important that voluntary severance does not become an employee right, but at all times remains a privilege granted at the discretion of senior management.

In NMMU's case, applications for voluntary severance were linked to showing evidence that a black and/or women staff member from within the institution would be available to step into the applicant's shoes. In exceptional cases, this rule was waived if such replacement employees were readily available outside the institution. This meant that voluntary severance not only reduced the likelihood of forced retrenchments, but, at the same time, served NMMU's aim of diversifying its staff profile. Formal retrenchments were only embarked on as a last resort after all other avenues of placing staff had been fully exhausted. In the end, less than 1 per cent of a total workforce of nearly 3000 staff members had to be retrenched.

Relationship between the vice-chancellor and the council

The final challenge to be discussed is that of the relationship between the VC and the council. The successful implementation of many an institutional restructuring has suffered because of poor or fraught relations between these parties. The reason why this particular relationship is highlighted is that council members, especially if the institutional restructuring takes place in a small city, are often approached directly by staff members and students and members of the general public with information regarding the many simultaneous restructuring activities which is either one-sided or blatantly incorrect. Unfortunately, such wrongly interpreted information can also easily find its way into the media, causing further unnecessary reputational challenges for the newly emerging institution.

During institutional restructuring it would be prudent for the VC to present a communications protocol to council for its consideration. Such a protocol should cover matters such as regular information sharing between the chair (and deputy chair) of council and the VC, either by way of meetings and/or telephone or email conversations; the submission of all restructuring communiqués to staff and students, and any media clippings regarding the institution to all council members; clarity on decision-making powers during crisis situations such as potential student or staff unrest; and the routing of all approaches by council members to staff or students via the VC or registrar's office in order to avoid any misunderstandings and crossed 'lines', to mention a few.

In NMMU's case, many of the above issues were agreed upon, but not in the form of a formal communication protocol. These agreements served to avoid many misunderstandings arising from wrongly conveyed or one-sided impressions by staff, students and the general public to members of Council. In addition, this really played a very positive role in maintaining a constructive and tension-free relationship between the Chair of Council and me. It also served to strengthen Council's governance and oversight role during the restructuring process.

Conclusion

Leadership and management during institutional restructuring are, on the whole, a matter of getting a few very basic, but nevertheless vital, issues right. One of the most important is that of striking an appropriate balance between 'people' and 'technical' restructuring issues. Ultimately, institutional restructuring will come to an end, but many, if not most, of the people who were present before the restructuring process began will also be present after it has been concluded. Any unresolved bitterness and feelings of animosity towards senior management and the institution as a whole could affect institutional performance negatively in the post-restructuring period. For this reason, it might also be prudent to introduce specific employee assistance programmes involving psychological counselling during the actual restructuring process. From the NMMU experience, the principal lesson in institutional restructuring was that, while sorting out the technical issues was essential, equally so was listening to, and talking and interacting with staff and students, even if it meant covering the same issues repeatedly.

Also, institutional restructuring should, where at all possible, deal with all the issues required for establishing a new institution or entity. Any unfinished business is likely to escalate in the post-restructuring period and become much more difficult to resolve. Institutional restructuring does, even in the minds of those opposing it, represent an opportunity to analyse and assess all institutional policies, structures, systems, relationships, practices, processes and the like. This opportunity should not be squandered, as it may not arise again for a very long time.

In NMMU's case, this was not fully achieved and there were some policies that still required formal harmonisation. However, these were mainly not essential for the immediate and functional operation of the new institution – policies such as a harmonised teaching and learning policy, or a harmonised policy on academic support for students. One matter which had purposefully been somewhat soft-pedalled was the development of a final strategic plan for the new institution, although some broad outlines of a new institutional identity and ethos were in place. This was done purposefully in order to give the incoming VC an opportunity to drive this process. Views within NMMU were divided on whether this was a sound approach or whether the development of an institutional strategic plan should not have been dealt with much earlier as part of the interim phase of the restructuring.

It was suggested earlier that, in some ways, despite the best project-planning efforts, institutional restructuring is very difficult to drive through by way of a number of sequential but separate subprojects, but rather requires a multidimensional approach where a large number of related issues are addressed simultaneously. This means that institutional restructuring invariably seems somewhat messy. This makes the clinical and unswerving adherence to the end goal by the institutional leadership critical, as, at times, many staff members and students will, in this somewhat messy environment, want constant reassurance that the 'ship is well and truly on course'. In fact, at the height of any institutional restructuring, some may simply follow the institutional leaders if they have sufficient belief and trust that they know what they are doing.

Did NMMU's restructuring meet all the requirements set out so far? The answer is probably largely yes, although, in some areas, mistakes were made through which many valuable lessons were learnt. Nevertheless, NMMU's restructuring process is regarded by many as being one of the more successful ones in South African higher education. When all is said and done, restructuring should, at least in part, be measured by the post-restructuring performance of the new institution in terms of outputs such as graduation rates, doctorates awarded, research outputs, increased third-stream income, and so on. In respect of such outputs, NMMU certainly is now performing at a higher academic level than its three constituent institutions did before the restructuring.

Without a doubt, this represented the most challenging time of my entire professional career. There were some real 'downs', but mercifully, the 'ups' far surpassed the number of downs. This represented a period of fresh insight into the make-up of other people, into my own person, into the importance of relationships, and into many of the leadership and management issues covered here.

Few experiences can be so satisfying, and, at the same time, so humbling, as to have worked with so many marvellously committed colleagues in putting the fractious history of the three institutions – UPE, PET and Vista University's campus in Port Elizabeth – aside, and, in the spirit and ethos of a new, free, just and democratic South African society, becoming part and parcel of establishing the NMMU.

chapter 7

Leadership challenges for research-intensive universities

Loyiso Nongxa

Professor Loyiso Nongxa was the Deputy Vice-Chancellor (DVC): Research of the University of the Witwatersrand (Wits) from October 2000. In April 2002, he was appointed Vice-Principal of Wits and, in November 2002, he became Acting Vice-Chancellor. On 1 June 2003, he was appointed the Vice-Chancellor (VC) of the University, a post he held for a decade until May 2013. He had previously gained invaluable management experience during his tenure on the councils of the universities of the Western Cape (UWC) and Cape Town (UCT), and later on the Council of Wits.

Born in October 1953 in Indwe, near Queenstown, Professor Nongxa is the youngest of five children. His father was a teacher, who became a principal, and his mother was a qualified teacher who stayed at home to raise the family.

Nongxa excelled in his studies throughout his education. He matriculated from Healdtown College, where he achieved the distinction of top matric student in South Africa in 1972. He obtained his BSc (Hons) from Fort Hare in 1976 and his MSc in 1978. In 1978, Nongxa became South Africa's first African Rhodes Scholar, and he went on to complete his DPhil in Mathematics at the University of Oxford in 1982.

Prior to taking up the post of DVC at Wits, Nongxa was a Professor of Mathematics at UWC from 1990 to 2000, during which time he was Head of Applied and Pure Mathematics for two years and then Dean of Natural Sciences for almost two years before leaving the University. Between 1986 and 1990, he was a lecturer and senior lecturer at the University of Natal, Durban. Prior to taking up the post at the University of Natal, and when he initially returned from Oxford, he taught Mathematics for four years at the National University of Lesotho, his field being pure mathematics and algebra, and his specialty group theory.

Nongxa has been a visiting research scholar at a number of universities over the last decade, including the universities of Colorado, Illinois, Harvard, Connecticut, Hawaii and Baylor. He is also an avid sports fan who, in his younger days, played rugby for the 'BaaBaas' team at Fort Hare.

This chapter is based on an interview conducted by Denyse Webbstock and Neo Lekgotla *laga* Ramoupi on 9 April 2014 in Stellenbosch.

When Professor Nongxa was preparing for his interview for the position of Deputy Vice-Chancellor (DVC): Research, he told us, he conducted some research on how one would approach a research-intensive university, and he came to the conclusion that one can shape the trajectory of the university around its performance in research. Nongxa got the job, and, while he was the DVC for Research, his predecessor, Professor Norma Reid, who was the Vice-Chancellor (VC) at the time, resigned. Because Nongxa was a Vice-Principal, and, according to him, by default, he became Acting VC of the University of the Witwatersrand (Wits). During that period, when Nongxa was Acting VC, he was asked if he was going to apply for the job. So he put his name forward, and he got the VC job. Reflecting back, Nongxa feels his career trajectory to the vice-chancellorship was in part accidental, and in part about the journey he almost unwittingly embarked on when he began to consider how it would be to lead a research portfolio at a university like Wits.

Research as the mission of the university

It is no surprise, then, that Nongxa's interest in research had shaped the way he came to see the mission of the institution. All universities have a research aspiration. No university, said Nongxa, could say they are purely a teaching institution, at least not in this country. It could be that institutions elsewhere, such as in the United States of America (USA), for example, with their community colleges and universities that award bachelor degrees only, would not put an aspiration to be better in research at the forefront. But that was not the case in South Africa. He believed, he said, that the challenges that South Africa faced required a response that is influenced by the research that the researchers conduct from the perspective of where they were located. He gave the example of energy, which has many dimensions; it has a science aspect to it, an engineering dimension, a political implication, an economic implication, it is linked to climate change, and so on:

All those issues have a South African perspective to them. To illustrate this: our energy generation is about 80 per cent coal-dependent, and coal and carbon emissions have a distinct impact on the environment. There-fore, balancing our sensitivity to climate change with the hard reality that South Africa really is dependent on coal, one then would have to, from the perspective of South Africa, think about the research that we do. We cannot simply follow what France, for example, is doing, which is based 8 per cent on nuclear energy.

What concerns Nongxa, therefore, is not just the fundamental research usually referred to as 'blue skies' research, but the fundamental research that addresses the questions that confront South Africans as a society. He had always believed that we couldn't depend on others to conduct that research on our behalf. He explained that infectious diseases, whether malaria, or HIV/Aids, or tuberculosis (TB), constituted another area where our researchers had to conduct that cutting-edge research which also addressed the collateral issues that South Africa faced concerning infectious diseases and poverty.

Nongxa envisioned Wits having a very strong research programme that would respond to the problems of society. He pointed out that it should be borne in mind that, as VC, he had come from the position of DVC for Research, where he had been asked by the institution to develop a strategic plan for research and to identify key areas for Wits to focus on. When he moved into the VC's office, he still had unfinished business transforming these research thrusts into flagship programmes for the University. Some of them had come to fruition over the years. For example, Wits now hosts the Centre of Excellence for Palaeosciences. The focus for highlighting that as a priority area for Wits, Nongxa said, went back to his time as DVC: Research. His time as VC at Wits was thus a continuation of the way he approached research as DVC.

A strategic plan called *Shaping the Future* was adopted in 2000 before Nongxa joined Wits. It had six or seven objectives; one of them was research and postgraduate studies. Under that section was a decision that Wits would identify priority areas that it would be known for. Nongxa's time as DVC was short but formative. He liked to say he was simply implementing the plan that Council and Senate had already formulated. His job would be developing criteria, looking at funding, and determining the critical mass and other crucial aspects necessary for success.

When he took this plan to Senate to show them the priority areas, there were academics that were upset about it. They felt, for example, that Mathematics was not obviously a priority area; but Nongxa felt that Mathematics was important as it is the basis for most scientific disciplines. A clause was then inserted to the effect that the University would support people in the research focus of their choice, but that, when the University pursued university-to-university partnerships, then, in the first instance, these would be built around the priority areas or existing relationships and collaborations amongst academics at the different institutions.

Financial challenges

What financial shape was Wits in when he took over, we asked him? Nongxa explained that, when he arrived at Wits, Colin Bundy had already introduced academic restructuring, which was a major development. This reorganisation had led to nine faculties being consolidated into five; and then about 95 departments were consolidated into 34 schools, following which devolution took place. There was an explicit decision taken that decisions about resources would devolve to the level where academic decisions were taken. As a consequence, deans had one-line budgets and they could exercise more power over allocating budgets. Currently, Wits does not have a central appointments committee; decisions about appointing professors are decided at faculty level, unlike at most universities in South Africa where there would be a joint council and senate committee responsible for appointments and promotions. Academic administration was also devolved to faculties. While first-years were still centrally enrolled, by their second year, students registered in their faculties; and from then onwards, all their administrative interactions would be with the faculties.

Nongxa found this created a big challenge for him as a new VC who had now to manage in circumstances of devolved administrative powers, but he had not been there when they were set up. When something contentious came up, the deans would say that it fell within the ambit of their powers rather than the VC's. He provided an example: "There was an Executive Director for Finance who was the head of the Finance portfolio at the University. The deans did not want to account to this person, because he reported to the VC." When he was new in the job, Nongxa said, he was not yet fully attuned to all the finance issues, and he had wanted this Executive Director to advise him as VC about the financial status of the faculties and about what was happening at faculty level. Nongxa said:

> It was something that was difficult to manage. Imagine it as similar to the different competencies that are either at the national, provincial

or local government level; that was something that one just had to manage. Now it depends on how one exerts one's authority as the head, in my case as the head of the University. One cannot throw one's weight around. After all, these people are your team. One has to continually try to strike that balance of co-governance.

Wits had instituted a process, which many universities also do, of a monthly financial review. The executive management would receive financial statements each month for every unit within the University. Looking at these statements, the executive management was able to say, "Faculty X, you are overspending on your HR [human resources]". In this way, we were able to have a collective discussion around the finances of the University.

Nongxa said he would consult around these devolved powers so that the expenditure and budgets and so on of the University, its financial health, could be overseen on a continual basis to see whether things were still on track, rather than leave oversight to a later stage. Knowledge of the financial problems that Wits was facing at that stage was crucial, since a great deal of money had been spent on restructuring. This had included the physical consolidation of faculties – for example, the Faculty of Education in Braamfontein was moved to Parktown, and renovations were undertaken. This meant that the University had had increasingly to dip into its reserves.

In addition, because people seemed to believe that the University had lots of money, budget managers never looked properly at what was in their budgets and what they had budgeted to spend. One example was the student financial aid fund: National Student Financial Aid Scheme (NSFAS). How was this best managed? At the time, students had to submit the necessary documents and the Financial Aid Office would analyse these and tell student X, for example: "You qualify for 80 per cent of your expenses." In many cases, the Aid Office did not know what the expenses of a student would be, because the different faculties charged students different fees and expenses. This meant that the University did not know exactly what it was committing itself to. The commitment was to a percentage of expenses, but the final figure often exceeded what the University had expected to pay:

Those allocating money to the students were not looking at whether their commitment was still within the bounds of what was in the budget. In 2003, when I was still Acting VC, we had committed more than we had budgeted for, by far, maybe by 20 million rand. So that was a challenge. The budget was something that was approved by

Council, and the deans would take cognisance of that. But then somebody in the Financial Aid Office makes a financial commitment on the basis of their assessment, and we couldn't afford it. So I guess that is why in 2004 we had student protests. We looked at the weaknesses of the system and said that we had to enforce the deadlines: if students did not submit all documents by the deadline, we would not be able to fund them. The students said that people in rural areas did not have a police station nearby, so were often unable to obtain an affidavit for submission in applying for student funding at university. So that was the challenge; we had devolved authority to spend, but those who now had the authority neglected to check the limitations of what they had in the budget.

Nongxa gave a second example of appointments that were being decided at faculty level, to underline the point:

When you set your personnel costs in your budget, you make the assumption that the finance committee of the faculty will work out the affordable staff complement for the faculty – so many professors, associate professors, lecturers, and so on – and you assume that all of them with be there for 12 months, that is, a full budget cycle. Then when somebody applies for, and gets, promotion, their salary scale increases, but the faculty has not taken that into consideration in the budgeting. So, again, when deans were not checking the decisions on, let us say, promotions, against their personnel budgets, we had a situation where the faculties were overspending on personnel costs. The Finance Committee and I had to introduce fiscal discipline; we had to get through to the deans that decisions had financial con-sequences that had to be kept in mind, whether they had budgeted for it or not.

Nongxa went on to say that he ended up having to develop a financial turnaround strategy that looked systematically at what the institution's income streams were, at the government subsidy, at fees, at personnel costs, at infrastructure, and so on. They also had to consider the major areas of investment for the University. He had to calculate how to maximise the share from the income stream; perhaps through improving fee collections or perhaps insisting that a third of the tuition fees must be paid upfront.

Nongxa explained that one of the outcomes of the turnaround strategy, and a major development, was the establishment of an Advancement Division, probably the first in South Africa. This was an instrument to leverage non-governmental funding, whether it came from the private sector, from the foundations, or the councils. It was also a way to capture the lessons learnt from the USA and Australian institutions that Nongxa had visited when he became VC. Between 2001 and 2004, Wits was running a deficit budget, but, from around 2005, the institution was generating healthy surpluses, and this trend continued up to the time that Nongxa left office.

Nongxa took the view that these challenges that Wits had faced were not unique to Wits; globally, institutions were experiencing similar challenges. His approach was always to look at how others had responded to them, and to distil best practice from the responses. If one wanted to grow one's research income, how had others done it? The strategy was then to train people so that they could emulate the achievements. In some instances, Nongxa said, he had tried to be creative, but, by and large, his response to challenges had been a systematic and scholarly one.

Reiterating a theme he had discussed earlier, Nongxa described how the presentation of the proposals was critical to their acceptance:

> Take, for instance, the question of research. I presented a strategy that said that we would have research priorities. Now, for argument sake, I knew that the people in the Social Sciences, had a different view, compared [with] the people in the Sciences of how research should be conducted. When I said we were going to have a priority in mining, the people in Mining Engineering might have thought: "This is us." But mining has different dimensions; there is also the social aspect of mining. The way one presents the proposal can either alienate some and not others, or it could bring people from different disciplines together, creating the possibility of learning about this complex issue from different angles.

Nongxa often heard people say that it was important for a leader running an institution like a university to have a strong team. For Nongxa:

> The term 'strong team' has different connotations. Is it strong technically? Is it strong in terms of leadership, and so on? I think I was fortunate that the DVCs and even deans, the majority of them, approached matters in a robust way. We would differ, but we almost always reached a common position about what should be done. I always thought I had a strong team, because we would thrash out things and come up with a strong position to defend; so it was strong in that sense. But it could have been strong in the sense of domineering: "You're a bully, you don't listen to us!"

Maybe I can give you an example. I wanted to merge Mathematical Sciences at Wits into a single school. I never got it right. People simply refused, and I could not prevail. Senate said they were not convinced. I felt this was right intellectually, but I failed to persuade them.

We asked Nongxa what provision he thought should be made for student diversity, for example in the case of students who came unprepared for university study. He confessed that, unlike research, this was not an area he had previously given much thought to. One of his good friends, the DVC for Academic Affairs, Yunus Ballim, then Chair of the Higher Education Quality Committee (HEQC), discussed things that he had never thought about – the pedagogy of big classes, use of information and communications technology (ICT) in teaching, and approaches to quality teaching. Nongxa remembered having a disagreement with academic officers in the early years of his vice-chancellorship about bridging programmes. Why, he had asked, if the students had met the requirements to be admitted, did they need bridging programmes? The academic officers were adamant that Wits had to have provision for some students to go through bridging programmes. They were experts in teaching and they would talk about the misconceived things academics did in their teaching. Not all academics were convinced, and they did not always take their advice, but rather continued to teach as before. For seven years, Nongxa said, he was fortunate to have had a good DVC for Academic Affairs in Ballim, and he would leave teaching issues to him. Whereas with research, Nongxa said, he would sit down, ask questions and even intervene where necessary.

Role of Senate, Council and 'managerialism'

Nongxa told us that the Wits Senate was large, comprising some 200 people. This included representatives of various university constituencies. His vice-chancellorship was during a period, still ongoing, where there were fundamental changes to the academic project, an increase in monitoring and evaluation, the requirements of the HEQC, and so on. Some academics simply did not see the need for, or importance of, investing time to understand these national developments. He said he came to realise that there had never been a meaningful debate about these issues in Senate. Some appeared not well informed about important documents like the National Development Plan (NDP). Partly as a consequence of this lack of understanding, Senate became angry towards the end of his term, because they saw management as simply a rubber-stamping machine. In addition, the academics did not seem to know that much of Senate's authority and power had been delegated to a range of committees: for example, academic planning and dealing with the HEQC. As a result, they felt disempowered, feeling that they were being bypassed. In the last year of Nongxa's term, management had a working group that specifically looked at how Senate was functioning and considered the things that made people feel disempowered.

We asked Nongxa to what extent he considered this to be a part and consequence of what has come to be called 'managerialism':

> [Laughs] I am chuckling, because people talk about managerialism, but they don't know what managerialism is! In some cases one doesn't have a choice. The HEQC requires compliance in order to register the university's qualifications. In a university, one has to have a budget, and then one has to manage that budget. 'Managerialism' and academic governance are poorly understood. People may not like it but we have to be accountable to the DHET [Department of Higher Education and Training]. Now [the] DHET [is] proposing biannual reporting, and maybe these new reporting regulations are going to become law. Wits will then have no choice but to comply.

He explained how Senate sometimes felt disempowered through the introduction of the devolved model, and that it was not being afforded the opportunity to engage properly with the academic developments at the institution. A lot of debates took place either at faculty level or within the subcommittees of Senate:

> Take appointments, for example, the criteria for promotion in the different faculties were not the same. Faculty X would say: "In order to be promoted from lecturer to senior lecturer, one has to have a PhD"; other faculties would say: "A PhD is not important for promotion", and so on. The standards were not the same. This presented a severe challenge. On the other hand, although certain authority had been delegated to faculty boards, faculty boards remained subcommittees of the Senate. Somehow, some academics did not see it that way, maybe because they did not participate in activities at faculty level but just attended Senate. Someone might raise a question about X at Senate, and you tell them: "But this comes from your own faculty!" I came to the conclusion that people didn't always pay attention to what was happening at faculty level, and consequently felt disempowered. There were all these powers devolved to the faculty and controlled by the dean. It is sometimes very difficult to convey the real power flow within the institution.

Nongxa explained his relationship, as the leader of the University, with Council as the governing structure:

I must say that I was lucky, because I had a good relationship with both chairs of Council that sat during my term. Edwin Cameron was the Chair for eight of the ten years I was VC, and it was he who recruited me. During that time, Saki Macozoma was the Deputy Chair of Council, so sometimes the Chair would delegate things to the Deputy Chair because he [the Chair] was away on business. Whenever I was unsure about something, I would ask for their advice or opinion. During my term we were also lucky because there were no groupings or blocks within the Council, which is the situation at some other universities, where the workers' unions or perhaps the students would lobby the ministerial representatives on Council. This can easily lead to the emergence of a block in Council that suspects management might be misleading Council, or might not be putting everything on the table, and so on. We never had that, never. I can't think of an instance when Council was second-guessing me as VC. They would ask difficult questions, and even say: "We don't understand this, could you please go over it again." But I would never get the feeling that they were second-guessing me about what we were proposing. They never just agreed with everything that we proposed, but one always got a sense that they had a good reason for why I had not persuaded them. Councils have representatives from outside the university, external people whose careers had most usually not been in a university. Some of them did not really appreciate that, as the VC, one was not the Chief Executive Officer who had the power to say: "This is the direction we will follow", that one could be outvoted by the Senate. One might want to do something, but the university community wants to do something else; and one would simply have to accept that. They did not understand that.

There were three Senate representatives out of 30 on Council; four or five from management; two students; and the SRC [Students' Representative Council] President.

There were, and possibly there still are, gaps between how internal and external people view the relations within the University, that, unless one had worked in a university, one would not understand them fully. External people did not appreciate the balance of power and authority that is traditional within the University; that one cannot simply tell department X that they should admit these students and not others. That is their decision. One cannot, as the VC, simply instruct them on matters like this; they have the legitimate power and authority to make their own decisions.

A good leader usually has guiding values. We asked Nongxa what values he thought a leader ought to embrace:

I can talk of some of the things I would remind myself of, which maybe were values to me. One was, I was always extremely wary of doing something behind the scenes where I might be caught out; for example in a lie, so that somebody could say: "You say this, but you are doing something different, you have a double agenda." I was always careful to avoid that. I felt that I should never do something that would come back to haunt me, that would embarrass me were it revealed. A second value was respect. Universities have a hierarchy; the higher one goes in the university system, there is this hierarchy which had a 'racial complexion', if one can call it that. The people who were more senior and respected in authority were mostly white and male. Then there was this tension between academic staff and support staff, which also had a 'racial complexion'; there were usually more females and black people amongst the support staff. Some people in the academic world would look down upon the support staff, and I would relate it to disrespect for black people and for women. I ended up consciously being more accessible to the support staff. Perhaps that did not endear me to the academics. But it seemed to me important to convey to those support staff: "You, too, matter in this institution." I came to rely on some people in the support staff. The Legal Officer, for example: I never managed properly to read all those big contracts, which nevertheless would bind the University, and, of course, would have to bear my signature. I had to trust her completely in terms of what she would suggest and what I was committing myself to. It reached a point where people in the University thought she was wielding too much power. In conclusion, I would say I consciously cultivated respect for people that might feel junior; and I consciously tried to be truthful. I just did not want to do things that would embarrass me as a leader.

The importance of integrity in a leader constantly arose during Nongxa's interview. We asked him to elaborate further:

At some stage I had to tell myself that I was not doing this job for myself, to say something about me. Wits was an important institution for South Africa; I was doing it for Wits. I always considered what would be in the interests of Wits as an entity that was going to be there far longer than I was. I always said I would put the interests of the institution above all else. For example, one could come into conflict with students about fees or with staff about salaries. But I said that, if I agreed to this, and perhaps didn't increase student fees, it was going to have an impact on the institution financially; just that alone was going to put the institution at risk financially. I consciously built up reserves. It would have been silly to take those savings and to put them into recurring costs, say into increasing staff salaries. That would have put the University in a hole so that it was not going to be able to balance its books. If there was a conflict between the interests of Wits as I perceived them, and the interests of anything or anybody else, I would prioritise the interests of Wits.

Nongxa had a well-known reputation for incorruptibility.[1] As he said to us again and again: "I could not compromise what I thought was in the interests of the University. The University has many constituencies: students; faculty X or Y; black; white; labour, and so on. I never felt party to any group. I felt that I always did things based on principle and logic and being objective."

Who deserves entrance to university?

Nongxa was of the view that, when one was responsible for the financial health of institutions, matters of transformation and social changes that were national goals were difficult concerns to address. He talked about the issue of financial exclusion of students and academically deserving students, and who should be supported. Nongxa gave his view:

It is a student who deserves to be given an opportunity because of being academically capable of making use of those opportunities by completing the degree, and who will go on to make a contribution to society – not that those without degrees do not. I came to learn that there were people and organisations that could in fact support those students, who would want to give opportunities to students who will provide success stories.

---

1   'Reflections on Professor Loyiso Nongxa as Vice-Chancellor' (2013) http://www. wits.ac.za/alumni/alumni%20news%20items/alumni201308/20861/news_ item_20861.html. Accessed 11 August 2015; Council of the University of the Witwatersrand (2013) 'Tribute to Professor Loyiso Nongxa' from http://freedommedia. co.za/witsblog/tribute-to-professor-loyiso-nongxa/. Accessed 11 August 2015.

This led Nongxa to look at ways of bringing these together: he set out to identify students who were academically deserving and needed support; whose application for funding the University could support. He initiated a students' finance project, which would identify funding for these students from the private sector or from government:

> Here is a funny story; I consciously developed a relationship with people who could fund students. Our students come mainly, but not exclusively, from the Limpopo and Gauteng provinces. I am from the Eastern Cape, and it so happened that the current VC of the University of Fort Hare was then the Director-General [DG] for the Eastern Cape province. I went to speak to him, and told him that there were students from the Eastern Cape who needed funding. He was in Johannesburg and I invited him to come to speak to the students from the Eastern Cape. This attracted the curious accusation that: "This Xhosa-speaking VC is only looking for students from the Eastern Cape. He must invite the DG from the North West province!"

Nongxa held the view that if a student was academically deserving, Wits would go the extra mile to get funding for that student. "One could have a student who owes fees from the previous year, yet they get funding for the present year. Wits would not allow them to register until they had paid their debt. So the University would give them a loan to pay that debt, so that they could register with the funding they had received."

Nongxa started a project called 'Targeting Talent' that searched for talented candidates and sought places for them in various universities across the country, not only at Wits. Through this project, Wits built relationships to inform the public that, if people knew of good students who had passed very well, they should not hesitate about bringing them to Wits, and the institution would make sure that they could enrol.

Relations with students and academics

Two of the ex-SRC presidents from Wits that were interviewed for the Council on Higher Education (CHE) Student Governance Project said that Nongxa was hard on them, but said that what was memorable about his vice-chancellorship was the Targeting Talent project that he had created. When we relayed this to Nongxa, he began to reflect on his relationship with the student leadership:

> There were two cases I recall clearly. The first related to a hunger strike by student leadership about a service provider catering on

campus; the second was that of the Dalai Lama. In the first case, the SRC President did not understand why I could not intervene when the catering company fired some of its campus staff. The reason I could not was because the catering service had been outsourced, and was not a matter for the institution. The students saw this as University hypocrisy with regard to the workers. In the Dalai Lama case, Wits organised a protest against the decision to deny the Dalai Lama a visa to visit South Africa. The students organised a counter-march protesting against what they described as hypocrisy by management, namely that there were other important issues that we had not protested against.

We asked Nongxa how appointments to the SRC were made: were these purely political appointments or were there requirements to qualify? He replied that the students were allowed to campaign under the banner of political organisations. The concession Wits gave the elected students was that they could have a reduced coursework load. Most of those that Nongxa remembered had graduated. Wits never had an SRC President who was elected for a second term. There were conflicts and disagreements around outsourcing throughout Nongxa's term as VC. In the early years of his term as VC, students were the most difficult constituency to deal with. In the last two years, it was the unions that had given him a hard time. Nongxa said he felt bruised, particularly around the salaries issue. But where he was most hurt, was when staff questioned his integrity. He explains:

> They said: "This man does not understand the workings of the institution; he has made a mess of this University." I had this sense that, sometimes, one can paint people in a particular way, with the knowledge that an observer would believe them because of the way they were portrayed. Often one doesn't need facts about these things. Popular wisdom has it that black leaders are bad, corrupt, crooks, and so on. Here is this bad black VC of this historically white university. Many people would simply believe that caricature. That's one of the things that really bruised me; that image that people have about black leaders they projected onto me, whether I was wrong or right. That was how I saw it.

It is interesting to note that some in the public domain, like historian R.W. Johnson, have a different perspective about Nongxa's term as VC of Wits:

As in any other career, a young academic needs to work away at the coalface, learning from experience, learning from their mentors and gradually accumulating a research and publication profile. If this career path is artificially cut short the result is that promising black faculty are rapidly made professors, deans or even vice-chancellors and thus loaded with administrative duties long before they have earned their spurs with research or, indeed, learned how to administer. There are a few of quite outstanding merit – for example, Loyiso Nongxa, Vice-Chancellor of Wits 2003–2013 – who serve with distinction all the same, though even Dr Nongxa's career as a mathematician inevitably suffered as a result from his accumulation of administrative duties at a too-early age.[2]

Conclusion

We asked Nongxa what challenges he thought the higher education sector faced today. A big challenge, he thought, related to reconciling the conflicting demands of different constituencies. Then there was the burgeoning demand for student places that he thought would be a growing challenge going forward. He recalled a time when enrolments of students were declining, but no longer. A large number of students now qualify to be admitted to university, and the choices about who to turn away, and on what basis, are going to grow more and more difficult to make.

Perhaps, Nongxa said, he would write a book about it. In the end, it boiled down to finances. A VC may have great ideas, "but if one does not have the resources to implement those ideas, nothing will come of them. It comes down to rand and cents! Anyone who has aspirations to be a successful leader must have a plan for that side of the equation; how is it going to be funded? It boils down to that in many cases."

Finally, we asked Nongxa what, in hindsight, he might have done differently in his leadership of Wits:

> I think I could have done more about strengthening relationships with other universities and constituencies that have come to mistrust Wits. I did not do much in relation to government departments like the DHET, the Department of Science and Technology, and the Department of Labour, which other VCs did, and did well. One might think one is avoiding undue influence on the institution. I think, now,

---

2 Johnson, R. W. (2015) 'The myth of transformation' from *politicsweb*, 21 April. http://www.politicsweb.co.za/news-and-analysis/the-myth-of-transformation. Accessed 11 August 2015.

one should build relationships with people even that one disagrees with. There were instances where people would say: "Loyiso is just a puppet; decisions are taken elsewhere!" People were certain that there were power brokers somewhere in the shadows. I think I could have done more to counter that mistrust.

The second is that I should have built a better relationship with the students, not only with student leadership. Sport at university, for example, is a big thing, but it was not something that I took an interest in. It was not on my agenda at all to be seen to be supportive of sporting bodies. I could have done more there.

chapter 8

Gender and transformation in higher education

Lineo Vuyisa Mazwi-Tanga

Professor Mazwi-Tanga was the first Vice-Chancellor (VC) of the newly established Cape Peninsula University of Technology (CPUT), after the merger between Peninsula Technikon and Cape Technikon in 2005. Her appointment came into effect on 1 February 2006 and she retired from this position at the end of 2013.

Her career as an educationist began during the volatile 1980s in several high schools in the Eastern Cape, where she taught, among other subjects, Mathematics, Science, Biology and Geography. In the 1980s, she joined the University of Fort Hare as a lecturer in Geography, where she also completed her master's degree. She was later awarded a Certificate in Higher Education Administration from Bryn Mawr College in Pennsylvania in the United States of America (USA). A research award took her to Durham University in the United Kingdom (UK) for an MSc in Climatology, and she was admitted as a Fellow of the Royal Meteorological Society. Thereafter, she joined the University of Cape Town (UCT) for a short period in order to carry out some research with the aim of completing a doctoral degree. While she was still engaged in this research, she was appointed as the Deputy Vice-Chancellor (DVC) responsible for Student Affairs at the Peninsula Technikon in Cape Town; and she started to work with Professor Brian Figaji, who was the VC of the institution.

Tanga remained in this post for the following ten years, until she became the VC of CPUT. In these roles, she has been involved in national bodies like the National Student Financial Aid Scheme (NSFAS), Higher Education South Africa (HESA) and the National Advisory Council on Innovation (NACI). She also served a term as Ministerial Advisor in the national Department of Education.

This chapter is based on an interview conducted by Denyse Webbstock and Neo Lekgotla laga Ramoupi on 11 March 2014 in Pretoria.

There was no direct route for Professor Mazwi-Tanga into academic leadership. Someone once asked her what led her onto the path of academic leadership. She responded by saying she thought it had a lot to do with mentorship. "Mentorship goes a long way. One learns a lot from those people who have led and who have led well" whether it was direct or indirect mentoring. When she was a lecturer at the University of Fort Hare, Tanga had a female Professor, Margaret Marker, who was her Head of Department. She admired her for her skills, her resoluteness, her hard work, and also for her forthrightness in making her voice heard on matters of equity and non-discrimination when, at the time, it was not popular to talk about such issues.

Tanga learnt a lot from the example of this female mentor. She learnt that one does not have to follow the popular view in order to do the right thing. This was at the start of the 1980s when transformation was just beginning to emerge as an important theme at institutions of higher learning. Information about the existence of discriminatory governance practices at the universities began to take centre stage, especially at the black universities where most students were African but where management was completely white and male. Tanga explained that there were other undercurrents as well, especially during the time of struggle. It was not always clear whether all staff members were genuine academics or whether some were working to further the apartheid system. It was a common occurrence to see some of the university lecturers dressed in military camouflage working alongside the police when there was strife at the University.

One of the consequences of this was that the staff (mostly black) joined the Union of Democratic University Staff Associations (UDUSA), a national organisation with membership at most universities. Tanga was nominated for funding – with Naledi Pandor who was at the UCT at the time – to participate in a programme for Women in Higher Education Administration and Management, in the USA, based at Bryn Mawr College in Pennsylvania, for about two months. It was through her participation in this international programme that Tanga became aware that women could have a greater impact if they themselves were in leadership positions. She began to see that women could make changes and could make a difference where their male counterparts in leadership positions were failing to do so, and she became convinced that women did not have to be hard-core politicians in order to bring about changes in the leadership of institutions. Her convictions regarding these matters started her on a journey that led her to enrol for a postgraduate course in Higher Education Policy at the University of the Western Cape (UWC). There she began to read and learn more about leadership, governance and management, as well develop an understanding of financial issues in the area of higher education.

Tanga cautions that, in South Africa, there is a tendency to take higher education leadership for granted. She argues that South Africa has not fully professionalised the development of leadership in higher education. Yet it is a complex profession. The tendency is to think that, if one has the qualifications and a deep disciplinary knowledge of one's academic subject, that one can be a dean, then a DVC, and then a VC. Tanga believes there are deeper issues to consider. HESA has attempted to address these issues, but does not have adequate funding, so the attempt is one of half measures. In many countries like the USA, the UK and Australia, these concerns receive more structured and professional attention. The result is that people emerging from these programmes are in a position to lead, and they are well prepared for the challenges that arise with the leadership of a university.

The other significant mentorship encounter for Tanga was with Brian Figaji. After working with Margaret Marker, Tanga had what she considers the privilege of working with Figaji, who was then the Rector and VC of Peninsula Technikon, at a time when she had very little experience in higher education management. The position of the DVC for Student Affairs at the Peninsula Technikon was her first senior leadership job. As was the case with Marker at the University of Fort Hare (UFH), she learnt about leadership, especially about the significance of integrity in upholding values, but also about ensuring that people understand that, if one has integrity, one is likely to be consistent. If one is consistent, then people begin to understand one's style and will follow if they buy into what one is trying to achieve. This became something deep in her that she always felt was an important aspect to uphold. It was not just reading about leadership but seeing it in practice, and witnessing the institution moving forward: that was something inspiring to see.

Professionalisation of higher education

According to Tanga, in the mid-1990s, issues of university management and financial stress, particularly in historically disadvantaged institutions (HDIs), became increasingly apparent. The student strikes were not merely driven by political considerations but by real bread-and-butter issues affecting the students. Universities were not well prepared to deal with these issues, nor did they know how to to pre-empt them.

Tanga also had the privilege of working with Minister Kader Asmal as his Special Advisor in the period 2001 to 2002, a period before the merger process was implemented. During this period there were institutions that were under financial strain, one of them being the University of Transkei (UNITRA) in the Eastern Cape province. What Tanga observed while involved with these institutions was the lack of capacity in deploying the available resources strategically. It was not only that the HDIs did not have endowments like the historically white institutions (HWIs), but the choices made in terms of resource allocation were not always well considered.

Her other observation was that there had been very little attention paid to upgrading infrastructure or conducting proper maintenance, with the consequence that the buildings in many HDIs were in a disastrous state – especially the student residences. While the issue of inadequate government funding was always a challenge, in many cases one could detect lack of effort on the part of the university. A situation like that, Tanga explained, raises the question about what is understood by leadership of a university. What does it take for an institution to work? How are the priorities for an institution determined? How should one set out to deploy the resources that are at one's disposal as a leader of such an institution? Although one cannot control the politicisation of the student body, there are things one can begin to get right to help set the university on a more stable footing, and which can help one to make progress. This is where capacity building and professionalisation of higher education management become important, Tanga contends.

Tanga believes that, at other universities at the time, the main challenge was an issue of governance, such as at the University of Durban-Westville (UDW), and at the Medical University of South Africa (MEDUNSA). At the University of South Africa (UNISA), the difficulties appeared to her to relate to a lack of understanding of the demarcation of powers between the VC and the Chair of Council. The Chair of Council thought he could occupy an office on the University campus and claim payment from the University for the time spent there. This conflicted directly with the authority of the VC on campus. Tanga used these examples to illustrate symptoms of malfunction in the system. Her proposed solution was the professionalisation of higher education leadership so that some of the issues mentioned could become embedded in a professional ethos, and so that people could better understand their roles, the rules and the basic principles at play. To a great extent, it was a matter of leadership, but it was also a matter of management, or, better yet, a combination of both. In many instances, the university leaders understood the one but not the other. In Tanga's view, management and leadership can both be learnt processes. One could not say they would be understood intuitively. There are certain principles that one has to master so that, if one applied them consistently, one would be able to get positive results.

Gender parity

Tanga had this to say about gender:

> The advent of democracy in South Africa brought along with it great expectations, both with respect to the government and at the local level of the institution. For the students as well as the staff, many of these revolved around redress issues. There was pressure both from inside and outside the institution. Students became more aware of their rights and began to expect more from universities; and staff became more organised, unionised, something that had not happened before. The only thing that was not addressed was the issue of gender equity. SRCs became dominated by African males; the leadership of the unions, too, became dominated by African males; and academic leadership became dominated by African or coloured males, depending on the institution. So, despite the pressures for redress, for some reason the issue of gender parity never came to the fore forcefully, and gender parity lagged behind.

We asked Tanga why she thought gender equity continued to lag behind while everything else was seemingly changing. "This is a difficult question," she replied. She felt it was critically important first to talk about the issue of oppression. She explained: "Oppression is like a bad disease that paralyses the oppressed; sometimes even though they have been cured they don't realise it." The first problem, Tanga continued, was that:

> African males, let me say black males, when the doors opened, … saw it as their opportunity to take up positions; and they were not going to be concerned about the position of women when they saw an opportunity to emancipate themselves.

The second problem with oppression, she felt, was that of apartheid. What apartheid had done was to create a very aggressive male species that, because they could not deal with the pressure they were experiencing from their bosses in the workplace, had to express their power by being dominant in their homes, which was not a traditional thing, as far as Tanga is concerned. Tanga contends that, when it came to the academic workplace, the male academics carried this baggage to the workplace and found it difficult to accord their female colleagues the same level of acknowledgement and professional respect. In other words, they implicitly assumed that women should not expect to be equal because they were women; they should not expect to occupy senior positions, for they were women after all. They should not aspire to be professors, and so on. So this patriarchal dominance, which was supposed to be addressed by liberation, actually had the opposite effect. "I suppose you can call that a perverse effect of emancipation."

Nonetheless, Tanga senses that responsibility is not only to be laid at the door of men. The academic women too had internalised their subservient position from the positions they had accepted at home, and they brought that to the workplace. Tanga observes that, even where you have two professionals as a couple, when there is a family crisis, it is assumed that the mother should stay at home and resolve the problem because dad cannot miss that important meeting, as though the woman is not also a professional. As a result, professionally, women tend to lag behind because the burden of sharing the responsibility was never balanced, even after so-called emancipation. Women then had to fight for recognition of their professional contribution or for opportunities to develop. At first, only those who were in environments where they had support at home could advance; or those who had a will strong enough to resist the temptation to be subservient, and pushed themselves forward. These were, and still are, few and far between, said Tanga.

While many believe that one cannot do very much without support at home, Tanga, on the contrary, is convinced that:

> One can! Sometimes if one cannot remove it, one learns to work around the obstacles. That is where leadership capacity building and empowerment and development would assist women in trying to look for the alternatives. But without some kind of intervention, some women will not see the possibilities of working around the obstacles, or finding a different route to still advance.

After a few years as a DVC, and drawing from the experience of the Bryn Mawr programme, Tanga had what she considered the privilege of receiving funding from Australia's Aid programme (AUS-AID) that allowed her to work with Dr Colleen Chesterman and colleagues from the Sydney University of Technology and other Australian Technology Network (ATN) member universities. They developed and offered a programme called 'Women Executives Development' (WEXDEV). Tanga imported this programme and worked in partnership with Australian university women to offer it in South Africa. The programme ran workshops that were facilitated by specialists from Australia who had been invited to South Africa. The workshops addressed issues of leadership in higher education, like the obstacles women experienced at home and in their professional life in the university. These workshops assisted women to work around these challenges and continue to develop their skills so that, when the opportunities arose, women might be ready to take up leadership positions. Some of the South African women she worked with included leaders like Mapule Ramashala and Neo Mathabe. Some of the women became deans as a result of their training in that programme; one of them is a DVC. A lot of it has to do with mental confidence:

> Someone once said that 50 per cent of the time, men who are average would stake a claim for a job, while women who are superior in terms of skills, qualifications and capabilities will not think that they are ready yet for the job. It is a psychological mindset; women require a greater push.

Tanga illustrated her point by referring to a study undertaken for the National Advisory Council on Innovation (NACI) on gender in the science, engineering and technology (SET) field (SET4 Women), which she formerly chaired. The committee was looking particularly at the sciences, where there was, and is, a lack of women involved in innovation. They found the same complex underlying the problem. So, said Tanga, the problem is broader than higher education: "Why are women not in the forefront of innovation and science research? The same reasons keep coming up again."

Tanga gave a further example from a meeting the Gender Mainstreaming Committee had attended in 2013 with the leadership of the National Research Foundation (NRF). The NRF was represented only by the two top men, the Chief Executive Officer (CEO) and the Chair. Even though the Committee had asked them specifically to bring their broad leadership, because the Committee wanted to have a conversation with them, they did not. Tanga and her Committee had written a discussion paper that they had sent to the NRF leadership explaining to them the issues they would have liked to discuss with them. The discussion paper started with statistics about the NRF's rated researchers by gender in the 20 years since 1994, which they felt had an impact on higher education. The Committee wanted to ask the NRF what they were doing about the gender situation. The Committee attempted to explore these matters with them, but Tanga could see that the NRF men were extremely defensive.

The example related to the challenges experienced by a young, upcoming female academic:

This young academic is publishing extensively and receives external research funding, and is doing very good work in an important area; that of teenage obesity in disadvantaged communities and looking at the schools in particular. The academic is a woman and her work is receiving international reviews. When she applies for an Associate Professorship, the Dean does not support the application. But the evaluators and reviewers feel she is doing good work and the independent reviewers feel the same way. So she appealed. The Appeals Committee ruled in favour of the applicant. When the matter served at Senate for final consideration, the Dean was still not prepared to accept the review results. The Senate, however, voted overwhelmingly in favour of the applicant.

Here is the moral of the story: the following year this same young academic applied for an NRF rating for the first time, and she got a C1 rating. C1 is an excellent rating, just below a B rating. The observation here is that female staff may find this very intimidating and would not persist and fight for recognition for fear of hostile treatment from their colleagues.

In Tanga's view, the pre-merger period presented an analogous predicament:

Before the mergers, at the time when there were 36 universities, I had observed and was disappointed that, between 1994 and 1999, there were only three women Vice-Chancellors: Brenda Gourley, Mamphele Ramphele and Connie Mokadi. I was, however, not surprised that that picture was such.

One of the comments I received, a few years after I was appointed Vice-Chancellor was: "But you managed to change that picture at CPUT", and my response was, "Yes, but at what cost to me personally?" I had inherited an institution where all the deans were males, and so, when a junior woman lecturer wanted to take up an opportunity to go and study, they would be asked, "Who is going to take over your teaching load?" It was never simply, "Yes good, go and do it. Go and finish your PhD, finish your Masters because it is going to improve our faculty profile." Whereas, if a male lecturer submitted his leave application it would be processed within two days because: "They've got to advance because they are playing a key role in the faculty."

When one has to change that scenario, one has to swim against the tide, sometimes risking one's own dignity.

Effective leadership and management

When we asked Tanga what she thought constituted effective leadership and management, she replied that she believed the role that the administration played to make the academic machinery work was critical. She cautioned that, if one did not have good administrative systems that were synchronised, then one was going to have hiccups that would lead to frustration for both the clients and the university that was delivering the service. The university would just not run effectively, and people were not going to have confidence in what the leader was doing. If one had administrative systems that worked efficiently, one could generate data with integrity that enabled a leader to know exactly where the university stood: whether the institution was doing well or badly, by the standards it set for itself, not necessarily in comparison with anyone else. The administrative systems were the backbone of the functioning of the university. The management systems helped the leader support the administrative systems. The management systems indicated how the leader should deal with the budget, and how to prioritise the budget in the key areas that a leader had identified as those requiring support:

> If one has got a strategic plan, one must ensure that one delivers on the plan. If one has identified the risk areas, then the strategic plan gives one a way of managing them. That is why I talk about the synchronisation between the administrative and management systems. When one has these building blocks and these elements in place, the question arises: Where is one going with this institution? How does one get it there? What is the strategy of getting it there? That is why I was talking about the integrity of the leadership, because the integrity of the leadership means that the elements in the system believe that one is taking them to the right place and that they can safely follow. The integrity of leadership is also being able to see when this strategy is not working and why; and being able to see how to remedy or improve on it. But leadership also enables one to learn from one's team and also the team to learn from the other elements in the system, because everyone is aspiring to the same thing. That's the theory. Then, of course, there are broad governance issues, which are about the relationships between the Department of Higher Education and Training [DHET], the Council, the leadership of the university, and how the powers are distributed, shared and related. That is why I said,

theoretically this is how things should work, but in every part of the system there can be challenges for a variety of different reasons.

The effectiveness of leadership and management in the university has been affected negatively by black economic empowerment (BEE). Tanga explains:

After the transition, between 1994 and 1999, the new awareness about rights and so on started a process that was very subtle, namely the issue of black economic empowerment. BEE in the economy broadly introduced a trend of youngsters who were getting tenders and were getting very rich very quickly. I don't think that was the intention of government, but that is how it transpired. The young impressionable minds in the universities started to wonder, "Why is it not happening to us? Why can't we be these young BEE moguls in the universities? Why are these companies being offered contracts and not those others; and how can we influence those decisions within the universities?" Then young tenderpreneurs emerged. That has destabilised the institutions. The politicisation aside, which I did not see as a negative thing, the tenderpreneurs have really meddled with the running of the universities. These are some of the complexities now that are emerging in higher education. The students want to have cars and live in posh apartments; and, if they cannot get their way, they can make the system ungovernable.

We then asked Tanga how students got into positions where they could influence decisions in the governance of the universities. She responded:

The Students' Representative Council [SRC] divides its work into commissions, which are a good thing. But companies tell SRC members who sit in tender commissions that, if they are awarded a specific tender, they will each get two hundred thousand rand. Those students naturally then do everything in their power to influence the outcome. It is no longer about student representation; it is now about individual interests and group interests. I am referring here mainly to private off-campus companies, but political parties can also try to influence decisions. That is why I say political parties and other political pressure groups can sometimes be dishonest. When students burn property on campus, political parties to which the student political organisations belong do not usually try to get to the root of the problem and find out what the causes are. In 2009 there was a huge strike at CPUT that took place without many noticing it. There was extensive loss of property and it was very disruptive. At the heart of their protest was the demand that the VC must go. I surmised that some of my Council members who did not approve of my leadership were behind it, but, of course, I could not be sure.

Institutional mergers

We asked Tanga what she thought, in retrospect, about the mergers:

> I am not convinced now, having gone through the mergers, that they were the ideal process for achieving redress. I think that, when the mergers were proposed, the intention was to change the apartheid higher education landscape to bring about institutions not based on apartheid principles and values. But mergers were such a difficult process that most universities that have gone through them have experienced some serious setbacks as a result. We were fortunate that our merger was between two institutions of the same kind, both being technikons, so our academic programmes were not that difficult to merge. Nevertheless, the evolution of universities of technology I don't think resulted in the same kind of treatment or recognition that other universities enjoyed, mainly with respect to funding.

At the time of the mergers, Tanga had been the Special Advisor to the Minister. We asked her to reflect on her experiences of that time:

> You must also understand that advisors have limited political influence, depending on the Minister that you are dealing with, of course. They tend to want you to work with the things they can get to, or that are not top of their priorities. But you do engage with them on the broader issues. One of the issues around the mergers that Cabinet was grappling with, was how the new government should continue with business as usual with respect to higher education when other areas of the system were being shaken up. A second issue, was that there were very few signs of change visible at that time. It seemed as though the historically white institutions that did admit black students did so on their own old terms. That at least was the perception. I suspect there was pressure on them to query these practices. But there was also psychological pressure on the government to the effect that the accumulated resources at some of the institutions were associated with largesse from big business. So here was a government under pressure to then build capacity in the historically black institutions; how should the environment be opened up to widen access to these

conspicuously better facilities and resources? I suspect that it was as a response to this complex challenge that the idea of mergers was hatched. Whether then the merger was the best tool to achieve that goal remains in dispute: some will say yes, others will say no. If you ask me, it is both yes and no; yes, because it did force some of the campus cultures to really change.

A good example of that cultural change, said Tanga, was the Cape Technikon. It was under black leadership at the time of the merger, as was Peninsula Technikon. The difference was that Cape Technikon was a historically white institution with a different cultural history. Tanga suspects that the merger forced each institution to look at institutional culture differently. The leadership had to ask itself, "What are the fundamental cultural imperatives and value systems that must be embedded in order to bring about a new entity, in order to make the merger work? As far as that is concerned, most of the merging institutions would have had to do that".

The challenges were not all the same. Consider the University of KwaZulu-Natal merging with the UDW and Edgewood College; consider ML Sultan and Natal technikons, now the Durban University of Technology (DUT); look at CPUT. The costs are difficult to measure, she said, as are the emotional costs, and the financial costs:

There were also mergers that happened only on paper, where the institutions continued to run in parallel with one another even though they were supposed to be a single integrated institution. In those cases, what has been the 'cultural gain'? One has only to look at the recent scandal at North-West University.[1] One wonders how such things can still happen so many years after the merger. Clearly, they have not been merged into a cultural form such that there is better diversity and better understanding of diversity. Some mergers have just not worked. Consider Walter Sisulu University, the result of a complex merger between Border Technikon, Eastern Cape Technikon and the University of Transkei. Unless they take a political decision to reorganise it, that merger will not work in its current form, even in the next 20 years. Consider also MEDUNSA and Turfloop, which were demerged after having been messily merged into the University of Limpopo. Again, that merger was not going to work. It is the same with

---

1   'NWU vice-chancellor steps down after nazi-salute scandal', 7 March 2014 from http://www.sabreakingnews.co.za/2014/03/07/nwu-vice-chancellor-steps-down-after-nazi-salute-scandal/. Accessed 11 August 2015.

North-West University; Potchefstroom has remained Potchefstroom and Mahikeng has remained Mahikeng. They did not really merge culturally or institutionally.

Tanga explains how, in her view, the merger of CPUT succeeded. It was decided that each of the campuses would host certain specific faculty programmes, and duplication would be avoided as much as possible. The argument for this was that students should have the same experience of the programme, taught by the same lecturers:

> Two lecturers may both be mathematicians, but the approach of one would be different from that of the other. The students of one lecturer would have acquired a different experience from those of the other lecturer. The new institution wanted students to say, "This was our experience", whether the students were pink, green, or yellow. Before, students used to say, "We are in Cape Town", or "We are in Bellville". I was sick and tired of hearing that every day. As the result of the relocations, we no longer hear students say, "We are in Pentech" or "We are in Cape Tech". Then one knows one has been successful, because, whatever they are sharing, whether failure or success, advantages or disadvantages, they are sharing together. Also as a leader, one is no longer able to discriminate against any of the campuses because one has now to distribute resources equally across the campuses.

Wellington campus used to have only one faculty, namely, Education. The University introduced other faculties, such as Agricultural Engineering and Hospitality, appropriately because the campus is located in a farming area and on a wine route. It is now a multi-faculty campus. When it was only Education, the campus had turned into an Afrikaans enclave because CPUT's Education Faculty there was Afrikaans. The leadership of the institution had wanted to keep it that way because their education programmes were in Afrikaans. It was not growing, but it was sustainable because there are Afrikaans schools in the area and that means there is a market for that Faculty. The new agricultural programme of this campus is doing very well. Those are the kind of decisions that the VC must make, said Tanga, for each campus to realise its full potential so that there are diverse programmes that can give students a much wider choice of careers. What the VC had realised with the Wellington campus was that it was assumed that to do education and Afrikaans one had to be white. To dispel that notion, Tanga said, they had to recruit Afrikaans-speakers who were not white:

Look at the Northern Cape province; the people in the Northern Cape think in Afrikaans before they think in any other language, whether they are black, white, pink or yellow. Find them, and they will enrol. It is quite a diverse programme now. One has to make those changes where you see they can be used to frustrate the process of transformation.

One of the things that Tanga felt strongly about was that the technikons were initially not funded for research. In the new consolidated system, all institutions are funded for research outputs at the same level. The universities of technology were, however, starting from either a low base or no base at all, both in terms of what they already had, and in terms of resources for conducting research and for supervision, and so on. As a result, there had been no emphasis laid on postgraduate degrees, or postgraduate degrees for staff members. So lack of supervisory capacity was clearly going to have an impact on their capacity to produce both research and postgraduates. When they became universities of technology, there was no redress funding for building up their research capacity in any significant way in order that they could pick up momentum:

Whenever I brought this up, the Minister would respond that the universities of technology wanted to drift away from their mission, which was to produce technical capacity and expertise. This would annoy me. I come originally from a traditional university, but I have grown to understand that the role of the universities of technology and the specific kind of research that they would appropriately do, does not have to be the same as that of the traditional universities. Nevertheless, it is of critical importance, because it is the kind of research that deals with issues of application and how that application can lead to innovation in a much more direct way than 'blue skies' research. As a country we are talking about economic development and lack of employment, and yet we don't see a direct channel that could assist with that process, at such a critical level.

Regarding the issue of research and mission drift, I once said to the Minister that I feel so sad when someone who has been an academic can want to put a silo between teaching and learning, or research and community engagement. For me, a good academic would be able to contribute to all three. It is not an either or, it is an and-and. What happens in the community can inform the research agenda, and what informs the research agenda strengthens the teaching and learning, because new theories emerge as a result of whatever research is done to either reinforce or to suggest new ways of thinking, of doing and of being. This has been the most difficult idea to bring home to the leadership in higher education. As a result, it gives some of the universities of technology a feeling of inferiority, of being treated in a lesser way than other institutions. I don't know what the solution to that is, but, I know for me, the determination of a new category of university, 'university of technology', was a policy advance, but I don't think there has been any follow-through in how best to position universities of technology. If one goes to other countries, these universities of technology are playing a critical and important role in advancing economic development. Just go to Finland, Sweden and Germany, for example.

The third aspect about mergers that Tanga discussed was the current shortage of universities in South Africa to carry forward the massification of higher education when the sector was in fact reduced from 36 to 23 through the merger process. The worst consequence, in her view, was the reduction of the 15 technikons to six universities of technology, despite all the talk about the 'inverted pyramid'.[2] For Tanga, what we should be producing and expanding is the mid-level of that pyramid. What is happening, according to her, is the other way round. Yet the national conversation is now about economic development, about job creation, and about innovation; all of those things that are so much more tangibly linked to this middle category.

Community engagement

Tanga explored some of the ways that can be used to deepen the impact of community engagement in the higher education sector. According to her:

> The challenge is one of understanding. Universities were historically elite entities that thought they were the custodians of knowledge; everybody must come to them, imbibe of what they offer, whether that was useful or not. I think the opening up of the world, globalisation if you like, is teaching us that sources of knowledge are not confined to the universities. Processes of knowledge creation and knowledge adaptation, knowledge usage, and knowledge management, occur in many places. The specific role of universities is to remain on the competitive edge. In order to do that, they have to learn to enhance that process, working with communities and learning with communities to enrich the universities and, in the process, to enrich the knowledge

---

2 Cloete, N., Fehnel, R. et al. (eds) (2002) *Transformation in Higher Education: Global Pressures and Local Realities in South Africa* (Juta: Cape Town).

of the communities. There is a lot of learning that needs to happen especially in South Africa around issues of community engagement and knowledge. We tend to assume that knowledge is value-free or has no value system. And yet that is not true. We are only now scratching the surface of what, for instance, 'indigenous knowledge' means to us as academics, or to the academic environment, and how significant that can be. What has bedevilled community engagement is the limited under-standing of how to work in communities, and with communities, to enrich ourselves in terms of knowledge production and knowledge management, building knowledge systems that are credible for both parties.

Tanga went on to discuss her own experience with community engage-ment at her institution:

Our approach was that we always had community engagement embedded in the academic programmes, but the issue was about making it more valued academically, not just making it a research area but building it into the credits of the qualification. We did not only value work that students had done with industries or government entities; we would also make them work with community-based organisations. They did some really fundamental work and learnt a lot. We would say to them that we wanted them to bring back what they had learnt so that we could insert these value-added experiences into the programmes; that is how we tried to build it amongst ourselves. I cannot claim that we have been completely successful, but there are places where we did have successes that brought us accolades for the work that we did in the area of community engagement. For example, we got international recognition from the Queen's Anniversary Prize, and the Tele-Network. Some programmes are more amenable to community engagement, and the academics vary in their commitment to it. Sometimes it requires somebody to be creative. The Information Technology Department, for example, worked with a community-based organisation on an HIV programme, and developed informative booklets with modules that our first-year students are now using in their multimedia studies.

From initial funding from Joint Education Services (JET), CPUT estab-lished the HIV programme as formally as possible. The University was fortunate to have the programme led by someone who is passionate about the subject of community engagement, Associate Professor Joyce Nduna, who had also been reading and writing about it.

The National Student Financial Aid Scheme

Another aspect of leadership that Tanga was involved with in higher education relates to the NSFAS. She was the first Chairperson of NSFAS after its establishment:

> I think it [NSFAS] is what I would call one of the best instruments for redress so far crafted. There are many young people that would not have had the opportunity to go into higher education were it not for this fund. I think the level of investment is quite considerable. The level of success has differed from institution to institution. Institutions that have been more successful are those which have had good administrative and management systems, because, when there are clear administrative systems, students understand why they qualify for funding and why they do not qualify. Because of our history again, what bedevils this is the dishonest way that some students try to get funding aid when they don't truly deserve it. If there was a system that could track the financial status of the family, perhaps through the South African Revenue Service database, so that, on the basis of good data, government could be informed accurately about the financial status of families, needy students could more accurately be identified and provided with financial aid. If we were able to do that, the money that government puts into national funding aid would be enough to cover the students that are in need, the students who are really in the low-income bracket. The problem, now, is that everyone applies for funding irrespective of the income levels of their parents.

Tanga suggests that what government can do in the meanwhile is to set the fundable income bracket just a little higher than it is at present to capture the students whose parents, although earning, presently fall between being eligible for an award and being eligible for a bank loan. Ironically then, it is the children of this slightly higher income level who are presently unable to afford university.

Then there is the problem of improper interference:

> We used to get calls from people in privileged positions, "Oh, but why did my nephew not get financial aid, or why not my son?", and you ask him, "What is your nephew's or son's name?" And when you explain to him why the applicant was ineligible (and bear in mind, this person is earning a good salary), he says, "I have another child who goes to Wits and I am also paying a bond". I used to say to them, "I understand that the net remains very low; but can you really tell me that the woman who manages to save R1000 from her R2000 domestic work

salary is richer than you? Because she cannot get a bond, she lives in a shack, does not have a car, commutes to work by train; are you saying I must deprive her son or daughter of financial aid? That is why her eligibility is greater than yours, because you have a bond, a car, and a cottage somewhere else. All she has is what she earns." That usually shuts them up. It happened often, and not only at CPUT, but many people shared the same experience.

Although Tanga stressed that NSFAS was a good scheme, her feelings were that there was room for improvement. She wondered whether it was not time for an extra, different scheme, where the student could take up a full loan which they could repay on completion of their studies or when they became employed. There was a need for support for merit-worthy students as well as indigent students. If the government or the banks were to establish such a scheme, then there would prob-ably be less pressure on the institutions. Tanga was quite exasperated with politicians who made irresponsible speeches from public platforms promising 'free higher education':

My goodness gracious, we have not had a free primary school education in this country because we cannot afford it! How can we promise free higher education? Such calls are simply irresponsible. Students go to these congresses at the end of the year, and they invite speakers, and they then hear this. Of course students will say, "Yeah! Viva! Viva comrade!" Then they come back the following year and say to universities, "We decided at our Congress that there shall be free education."

What also irritates Tanga is the inconsistency of government. The government would tell an institution it could fund the university, say, ninety million rand, according to the formula it used; but there was no more money. Then the students would dance (toyi-toyi) a few times, depending on the Principal. The officials would come; they would meet with the students and ask why the university was not controlling their students. The students would say they needed money, and the government officials would say, "We will assist you."

The next day, they give the institution thirty million rand more. The question then arises: where did that money come from? If it was not budgeted for, why was it not budgeted for? If it was not allocated, why was it was not allocated? If there was no money, how suddenly did the officials come up with thirty million rand more? That is the inconsistency. The students see this; they are smart. Those are some of the difficulties that arise from both inside and outside. If the administrative systems are weak, then the students will exploit them.

Achievements major and minor

We asked Tanga to tell us about the aspects of her leadership that she was most proud of.

[Laughs]. That is difficult to answer. I think, for me, the greatest thing was to leave an institution that was financially viable; that we had maintained student success rates that were just above the national average; that we had started to grow our research output, not signifi-cantly in comparison with traditional universities, but as a university of technology that had started from no base, we had come to see quite significant expansion over time, especially in the later stages of my tenure. I am very, very proud of that.

The second aspect she was proud of concerned transformation:

I am proud of the transformation successes that we were able to achieve: integration in terms of staff equity, in terms of gender equity. I can look back and say I can see a visible difference there. Lastly, the development of staff profiles with respect to their academic qualifications is something that I believe has been achieved. The resources I had been able to fight for and bring into the University to enable the University to physically grow; the research and teaching spaces; student accommodation, although this remains a challenge. When I look back, I see there has been growth in some areas.

We asked her whether there were any things she might have done differently:

There are many, I am sure. Under the circumstances I have described, I think, though, there was very little I could have done differently. Had the circumstances been different, I would have been more aggressive in terms of driving funding for staff release, funding for staff development. I think those are the areas that require work. Under the constraints I have already outlined, I think the University has, broadly speaking, done very well. The team that I worked with did me proud, I must say.

There are areas in student development, outside of the academic environment, where work also needs doing. We did not master a clear development trajectory for our students. I think there could have been more extramural activities to empower and enhance our students. The other area where I had not done well, was in ensuring that student leadership was more integrated, did not swing from one extreme to the other; became integrated in terms of race and gender. Those are the areas that I think had not been as successful as one might have liked, especially in the light of the new South Africa.

Higher education leadership challenges for South Africa

South Africa continues to face challenges of higher education leadership, and Tanga offered these views:

> I think we have not quite figured out how best to reorganise the sector. Perhaps I have not fully understood the *White Paper on Post-School Education and Training* that has just come out.[3] I am not sure if that is going to yield the desired results, because I think we have clustered too many things under one roof. There is Adult Education that has been placed as part of the post-school landscape. I am not sure if all Adult Education is at the post-school level, and yet it is now to be considered as if it is at that level. We have not looked at the curriculum of the further education and training band in a clear enough way to understand how it articulates with the world of work, or how it articulates with higher education for those who want to proceed. I am not sure if the SETAs [Sector Education and Training Authorities] should be part of the post-school system, or how they should be factored in in a manner that is going to assist the development of the system. We don't know whether they are funding agents or development agents or agents that ought to run programmes in their own right. These are things that are not yet clear in the White Paper.

The second challenge Tanga offered had to do with leadership itself, not at the university level but at the government level:

> I worry about the capacity of the Department of Higher Education and Training to deliver on its mandate. There are people in the Department who have been appointed in acting capacities for a very long time in positions that are critical. It is difficult for staff in acting positions to take firm decisions on important issues. I also don't see appointments to that Department of people who are knowledgeable and experienced, such that they can speak with authority on the issues. Nor does a high

---

3   Department of Higher Education & Training (DHET) (2013) *White Paper for Post-School Education and Training – Building an Expanded, Effective and Integrated Post-school System.*

rate of staff turnover do anything to stabilise the Department. As a result, key bodies like HESA don't find it easy to engage meaningfully with the Department or the Ministry. I attribute that to the fact that they are probably very thinly spread in order to cover all the bases. HESA, as the body speaking on behalf of the universities, finds it difficult to engage on policy issues. Sometimes policy processes are not followed, as one would expect. You hear that an announcement is to be made, then you are asked to comment on a policy position that is already on its way to Parliament. There is no engagement with the sector or the people who are supposed to implement those policies. It becomes a challenge to deal with this, because, if you make a comment about this process, you are seen as challenging the Department.

I am not sure if there is even openness to attempt to understand the problem. I am not suggesting that everyone who works for the Department should have worked at a university, but, if one works with the university sector, it would help to have a broader understanding of the sector. My sense, for instance, is that the Department should provide the continuity; the Minister, like all political actors, comes and goes. The people who must provide continuity are in the Department, so we need to beef up the Department so that, when there is a new Ministry, they are able to inform the new incumbents knowledgeably. When both are not fully informed, we are all in trouble.

Dealing with constituencies

Tanga was asked which constituencies she found most challenging to deal with:

I have not found any constituencies difficult to work with as a constituency. I used to say to people, in spite of some of the difficulties we had in the public domain, that I never had a single strike at CPUT during my tenure as VC, not by my own staff. The labour issue that was there was from workers of a contracted company who were unhappy with their employer but staged their unhappiness on campus. I never had to deal with a strike by my own CPUT staff. Again, having come to understand where student issues came from, I would say the trouble did not come from students; it came from individuals who had their own issues that they were dealing with.

I imported some of the processes I had learnt during my experience as a DVC: Student Affairs to my portfolio as a VC. The most important was: if you don't give students platforms to talk to you as the leadership, you are not going to know their concerns. I would insist on quarterly meetings with the student leadership, and I would say, "It is an open process". I would have preferred that we talk more about higher education, but I was prepared to talk about anything that concerned the students. So we would discuss and sometimes fight, and so on. But it all helped, because I then knew where the red flags were, and I could inform those who should have been dealing with them, to address them before they became problematic for the running of the institution.

Having systems in place also helped me to maintain financial stability. When I took office, I said that there were three things I needed to look into. I needed to ensure financial stability; ensure academic integrity; and ensure that the institution remained viable. As a result, these things helped me to know who was doing what and where. Some people did not like it; they said I was micromanaging them, but it helped me to know where the finances were. I never had qualified audits in all the years I was responsible for CPUT. I am not saying there were no problems, but, if you get to be involved in all the operational areas of the University, you get to understand how things work. So constituency-wise, I cannot say there was any particular difficulty.

Broadly, higher education leadership is difficult. This cannot be attributed to a single issue. It is difficult because of external issues; it is difficult because of the resources that are limited, which is not unique to higher education; it is difficult because the need out there is so great; it is difficult because the institutions like CPUT, with mostly black students that come from disadvantaged communities, carry the burden of poverty, unlike institutions which can draw middle-class black students. Even though those institutions do have black students, those students come mostly from affluent families. If you ask a student from my village if they will ever apply to UCT before that student applies to CPUT, they will not, because they assume UCT is outside their league. A student who applies to UCT has a father or mother who is a graduate and has said, "I want my child to go to UCT". So they are dealing with a different kind of constituency and the burden of poverty, therefore, is lighter. I am using UCT purely as a hypothetical example. I suspect, though, that most HDIs feel that burden. Nevertheless, it need not result in chaos!

Conclusion

Finally, we asked Tanga what advice she would give to a newly appointed VC of a university today:

First, I think the first challenge is to understand the team that one has to work with. Secondly, understand what the governance of higher education is about, what the VC or the Chair of Council is supposed to do, because I think, in many instances, that can also bedevil the issue of where the boundaries lie. Thirdly, make sure that the administrative and management systems are in place. Make sure that the backbone is in place. If it is not, set it up as soon as possible.

Fourthly, do not try to change everything at once, on day one, because you are going to cause chaos. Prioritise. I know it can be difficult, because circumstances do not always permit you the space you need. When your top team retires all at the same time, for example, then you have a problem. That is why I was saying: try to understand your team, because your team is going to be your pillar. Do your very best not to alienate any member of your team, unless that person alienates you. Your duty is to bring everybody in. Your duty as a VC is to know everything. The buck stops with you.